Salted With Fire

Salted With Fire

Unitarian Universalist Strategies for Sharing Faith and Growing Congregations

Edited by Scott W. Alexander

Skinner House Books

ISBN 1-55896-289-1
Printed in Canada.

Production Editor: Brenda Wong
Copy Editor: Linda Hotchkiss Mehta
Designer: Suzanne Morgan

10 9 8 7 6 5 4 3   / 99 98 97 96 95

Library of Congress Cataloging-in Publication Data

Salted with fire : Unitarian Universalist strategies for sharing faith and
    growing congregations / edited by Scott W. Alexander.
        p. cm.
    Includes bibliographical references.
    1. Unitarian Universalist churches—membership.   2. Church growth—
Unitarian Universalists.   3. Evangelistic work.   I. Alexander, Scott W.
BX9842.S29   1995
289.1'32—dc20   94-40201
                                                                    CIP

To William Burnside Miller (1948-1994)

It is with both gratitude and sadness that I dedicate this book to the memory of my colleague and friend William Burnside Miller. Bill's untimely death at the age of forty-six cut short a distinguished career in the Unitarian Universalist ministry. His commitment to our Unitarian Universalist movement, competence as a parish minister, and passion for building strong and growing churches were truly exceptional. As it moves toward the next century, our living faith tradition shall miss his intelligent energy, and I shall miss his unquenchably warm and enthusiastic presence.

Contents

Affirmation

In a world with so much hatred and violence,

> WE NEED A RELIGION THAT PROCLAIMS THE
> INHERENT WORTH AND DIGNITY OF EVERY PERSON.

In a world with so much brutality and fear,

> WE NEED A RELIGION THAT SEEKS JUSTICE, EQUITY,
> AND COMPASSION IN HUMAN RELATIONS.

In a world with so many persons abused and neglected,

> WE NEED A RELIGION THAT CALLS US TO ACCEPT
> ONE ANOTHER AND ENCOURAGE ONE ANOTHER
> TO SPIRITUAL GROWTH.

In a world with so much dogmatism and falsehood,

> WE NEED A RELIGION THAT CHALLENGES US TO A
> FREE AND RESPONSIBLE SEARCH FOR TRUTH AND
> MEANING.

In a world with so much tyranny and oppression,

> WE NEED A RELIGION THAT AFFIRMS THE RIGHT OF
> CONSCIENCE AND THE USE OF THE DEMOCRATIC
> PROCESS.

In a world with so much inequality and strife,

> WE NEED A RELIGION THAT STRIVES TOWARD
> THE GOAL OF WORLD COMMUNITY WITH PEACE,
> LIBERTY, AND JUSTICE FOR ALL.

In a world with so much environmental degradation,

> WE NEED A RELIGION THAT ADVOCATES
> RESPECT FOR THE INTERDEPENDENT WEB
> OF ALL EXISTENCE OF WHICH WE ARE A PART.

In a world with so much uncertainty and despair,

> WE NEED A RELIGION THAT TEACHES OUR
> HEARTS TO HOPE AND OUR HANDS TO SERVE.

Scott W. Alexander

Introduction

For every one shall be salted with fire. Salt is good; but if
the salt has lost its saltiness, how can you season it? Have
salt in yourselves, and be at peace with one another.
                                        —Mark 9:49-51, NRSV

Suddenly, a new *evangelical* spirit is stirring within Unitarian
Universalism! That's right, I just used the dreaded word "evangelical" that for generations has seldom crossed religious liberals' lips except when we were dismissing the proselytizing of
fundamentalist televangelists. Despite the fact that both the
Unitarian and Universalist sides of our proud heritage have had
periodic outbreaks of evangelical fervor, over recent decades
Unitarian Universalists have been content to sit back, refusing to
proselytize, waiting for those who were "Unitarian Universalists
without knowing it" to stumble upon us by chance. As Harvey
Joyner, Jr., bemoans in "The Bold Witness":

> [W]e have a vision for creating a more loveable and
> liveable world . . . why are we not out there telling any
> and everyone in our community about it? Instead of
> ridiculing fundamentalists for their seemingly bound-
> less zeal and overly simplistic answers, why are we
> smugly content with our self-description as "the best
> kept secret in town?" . . . Our cause is for the enhance-
> ment of human dignity and for creating inclusive circles

Introduction

of love. That is our gospel. That is our good news. Isn't it about time that we go tell it on the mountain?

Many UUs are finally moving up the mountain, with a new (and, to some, surprising) evangelistic passion to share their faith and grow their congregations. Scores of Unitarian Universalist leaders (both clergy and laity) are talking openly and enthusiastically about evangelism (both personal and institutional) and why it is so imperative in this moment of human history that we practice it, bringing as many people as we can to the noble and living faith that is Unitarian Universalism.

From its New Testament roots describing the efforts of those impassioned believers who wrote and spoke about the religion Jesus taught, evangelism today is about sharing the "good news" of one's faith tradition. As John C. Morgan defines it for us in his essay "Shout It Out Folks: We're Evangelists, Too!":

> Evangelism is sharing our dream with others in order to transform the world. . . . Evangelism begins with a dream, a vision that has power to claim some ultimate demand on our lives. . . . I believe that there is power and purpose in our Unitarian Universalist dream to shape the world around us into one more loving and just. . . . I believe that the times are ripe for our saving message, because there are many people who would share our dream if we would let them know we are here.

Something that many Unitarian Universalists have been slow to recognize and embrace is that the *evangelical techniques* (the *strategic methods* for institutional growth) so successfully employed by religiously orthodox Christians *stand quite independently* from their fundamentalist message. Religious liberals can learn from and employ these evangelical methods without in any way adopting, mimicking, or supporting their orthodox message. Many of the essayists in this volume fully understand this dichotomy between evangelical method and message and describe how they have enthusiastically adopted (and adapted) the evangelical techniques of religious conservatives to trumpet and spread our *liberal* "good news."

Perhaps one of the few positive things that has resulted from the aggressive activism of the radical religious right in what social commentators have come to call "the culture wars" is a renewed sense among Unitarian Universalists that they have a unique and *valuable* religious vision to offer others. Whether or not we welcome these battles that have broken over us, the culture wars are all about the struggle in the public square between competing (theological and ethical) visions. And we must realize that it makes a great deal of difference, to us and to the rest of humanity, which visions triumph in the struggle.

As religious education evangelist Sophia Lyon Fahs reminded us earlier in the century:

Some beliefs are like walled gardens. They encourage exclusiveness, and the feeling of being especially privileged.

Other beliefs are expansive and lead the way into wider and deeper sympathies.

◆ ◆ ◆ ◆

Some beliefs are divisive, separating the saved from the unsaved, friends from enemies.

Other beliefs are bonds in a world community, where sincere differences beautify the pattern.

◆ ◆ ◆ ◆

Some beliefs are rigid, like the body of death, impotent in a changing world.

Introduction

Other beliefs are pliable, like the young sapling,
ever growing with the upward thrust of life
(from "It Matters What We Believe")

As the radical religious right has unashamedly attempted to influence both public policy and private morality to singularly reflect *their* theological and moral perspectives, religious liberals have slowly awakened to the fact that we remain silent and hidden about what *we* believe and dream at our own peril. If we are not bold and caring enough to stand up in the public square and (without arrogance or vitriol) affirm what it is *we* believe and what dreams command *our* loyalty—then by default it will be the beliefs and dreams of *others* that will influence and instruct the shape of our society and the lives of those around us.

Unitarian Universalists, after a long period of continuing to hide our light under a bushel, have finally realized that the stakes in the current culture wars are terribly high. We cannot afford to sit on the sidelines and let others be the only ones proudly and passionately offering a vision for the human future. In a process not unlike what psychologists call "reaction formation," the radical religious right's aggressive ability and willingness to clarify its beliefs and values has motivated Unitarian Universalists to once again clearly articulate what it is *we believe*, and how it is we are then called to *live* our humane and healing vision.

Yet it is terribly important as we evangelistically work to spread our faith and build our congregations that we dispel the notion that "We have created a new utopian religion." True evangelism, for liberal or conservative, is not about arrogance and absolutes, but about sincere devotion to a dream for the human enterprise that informs *and* transforms our own lives and other lives around us. Our Unitarian Universalist "good news" is a principled religious message that has the power to humanize society and persons in healing, saving, responsible ways—but only if it is boldly spoken, eagerly shared, and passionately lived by those of us who claim this proud heritage.

Eight Key Guidelines for UU Growth and Evangelism

This book is comprised of twenty-two essays written by a group of unashamedly evangelistic Unitarian Universalist leaders from all over the continent—men and women who are passionately committed to the growth and extension of Unitarian Universalism. As I compiled these essays, I've struggled first to see and then understand the "big picture" of this new wave of evangelism and growth that is sweeping our movement. I've done background interfaith reading on church growth and evangelism strategies, visited many thriving UU congregations, had extensive conversations with our own UUA Extension Department, and contacted most of the Unitarian Universalist ministers serving rapidly growing (and spiritually lively) congregations—many of whom, incidentally, ended up being contributors to this volume.

What emerged from these diverse sources were *eight key factors* that seem to enhance, enable, and engender Unitarian Universalist growth and extension. Some of these factors are identical or very similar to those that would be found in conservative or mainstream circles, but others are unique to our UU needs, culture, and style. It is obvious that when we speak of evangelism for Unitarian Universalists, we are talking about something quite distinct from the manipulative style of many televangelists. When we share our faith and grow our congregations, it must always be in ways that reflect and enhance the principles, spirit, and style of our free faith.

If we are to successfully evangelize and grow, Unitarian Universalists must give attention to the following guidelines.

1. *Have the spiritual conviction (on the part of both clergy and laity) that we have a "saving gospel" that commands our loyalty and compels us to share it with others.*

Without a heartfelt spiritual conviction that we have precious "good news" to share with the world, no evangelism/ growth strategies or techniques will do any good. We need the

Introduction

institutional clarity and conviction of my colleague Patrick O'Neill who writes, "I am not very ambiguous about the value of our church. I see our Unitarian Universalist church as an agency of great principles: an institution that promotes tolerance and social justice, hope and reason, service and caring connection in a world where such commodities of the spirit are fragile and all too scarce."

And we need the *individual* clarity and conviction of Harvey Joyner, Jr., "The *sine qua non* for 'telling the good news' is the personal faith of the evangelist. If one does not have one's own faith house in order, one is not at all likely to want to be an evangelist. You cannot share your faith if you do not have a faith to share." Without genuine, heartfelt spiritual conviction, nothing is possible.

2. Challenge both ministers and laity to confront and change the array of deep-seated and long-standing UU cultural norms and assumptions that are barriers to growth and evangelism.

We need to radically change both our personal and institutional attitudes about growth and evangelism as the first step to allowing both to happen within our movement. Despite occasional protestations (and actions) to the contrary, for several decades now Unitarian Universalists have both thought and acted in ways that ensured that our faith was not successfully spread and our congregations did not (significantly) grow. William Burnside Miller put it very bluntly in his essay "Dangerous Myths":

> Perhaps the most dangerous of all [Unitarian Universalist] myths is the belief that we want to grow. . . . [G]rowth is the farthest thing from the minds of some liberal religionists. Many of our societies operate as private clubs open to members only. After all, if you have discovered 'Truth,' 'Beauty,' and 'Right' and know that only a small elite can possibly attain that goal, then surely you do not want to be sullied by the intellectually, spiritually,

or culturally unwashed. We smugly congratulate ourselves on our rejection of proselytizing, grandly affirming
a gracious tolerance of differing points of view. We then
sit content with our small numbers, knowing that our
way can only appeal to people who are truly superior. . . .
After all, if small is beautiful, then tiny must be terrific.

Only by systematically confronting and changing our "anti-
growth/evangelism" UU cultural norms will we ever create the
possibility for significant institutional and individual evangelism.

3. *Engage in intentional strategic planning for growth, at both
the congregational and denominational levels, once a genuine
consensus for such growth is achieved.*

If our movement is to grow significantly, it will be because of
intense, careful planning on both the local and denominational
levels. By studying both individual congregations and entire
faith groups that have achieved sustained growth, we know that
they do not grow by magic (though there are mysterious and
magical components!), they grow by purposeful, strategic planning. Analyzing the significant growth of the church he served,
William Burnside Miller observed, "Much of the success . . . has
to do with the fact that both the members of the congregation and
I desired growth. We honestly shared a common goal and then set
about to realize it with great intentionality." Regardless of demographics, any Unitarian Universalist congregation that *seriously
wants* to grow can plan for (and then celebrate) that growth.

4. *Empower the laity to be partners in the ministry of the
congregation, living their Unitarian Universalism in the church
and beyond.*

Unitarian Universalist congregations that want to grow need
to shift their understanding of *what* ministry is, and *who* does it.
In growing churches, ministry is a *partnership* between effective
professional ministers and lay people committed to sharing in
the work of the church—both within and beyond its walls. Lay

Introduction

empowerment means having ministers who are, in the words of Terry Hershey, author of *Young Adult Ministry*, willing and eager to "give the ministry away" so that laypersons can serve the mission of Unitarian Universalism in their local communities and beyond. As Barbara Wells writes in her essay "Giving the Ministry Away":

> Why is [lay] empowerment important for large, growing churches? One answer is obvious. No member of the clergy can do every bit of the pastoral, preaching, teaching, prophetic, and organizational ministry in any church. . . . Giving the ministry away is like pouring water out of a cup that never empties. True empowerment means there's plenty to go around for everyone.

Congregations that grow do so because everyone has been empowered to participate directly in achieving the local (and global) mission of his or her faith tradition.

5. *Create full-service, seven-day-a-week, twelve-month-a-year congregations.*

We must have vibrant, diverse institutions in order to respond to the varied needs of the baby boomer generation now actively "church shopping" in astounding numbers (recent studies indicate that this "demographic window of opportunity" for religious groups will shut in just a few years). It has been widely documented that "boomers" want a church where they can be active and involved—a place where they can ground their lives, religiously raise their children, and find meaningful ways to express both their compassion and spirituality. In "To Grow a Serving Church," Susan Milnor writes:

> The work we do in our Unitarian Universalist congregations should be so important that we cannot turn it off for months or even weeks. . . . To be 'full service' means to provide opportunities for members and friends to de-

velop spiritually, to grow emotionally, to participate in
efforts to make the world more just, to find God, to mark
the great passages of life, and to create and celebrate the
"beloved community." . . . Many of us require a critical
shift in our thinking, however, before we can even conceptualize the full-service church.

Let there be no doubt about it, if we do not provide the present
baby-boomer generation with the full-service churches they seek
(offering many small educational and service groups where they
can find a niche for themselves), they will go somewhere else to
get it!

6. *Encourage congregations to have a visible, effective, and
concrete "service mission" in their local communities and the
wider world, which unmistakably reflect our Unitarian Universalist principles and values.*

The congregation that primarily looks inward for the discovery of meaning, wholeness, service, and spirituality (and does
not move out beyond its walls to visibly *live* its religion in
the wider community) will not experience growth and depth.
Recent studies indicate that the "church shopping" baby-boomer
generation fully appreciates the truth that *service to others* is
an essential component to a full and responsible spiritual life.
One analyst says "boomers" are looking for churches to help
them "find avenues to express their compassion" in a troubled
world. As UUA President John Buehrens says in his essay, which
describes the resurgence of service outreach projects in growing
UU congregations, "Social ministry projects are being seen as
opportunities not just to change the world, but to change ourselves as well. . . . Service projects should not be disparaged as
'mere Band-Aids on open wounds.' . . . Religious people, to be
responsible, must try to respond—for the sake of their own souls.
A good program of congregational social ministry creates hands-
on opportunities for spiritual growth through service to others."
An inward-looking church that does not empower its ministers

and laity to take their faith to the streets in service of others is a church that cannot grow in numbers, responsibility, or depth.

7. Encourage congregations to provide quality programming and worship.

In his essay, "Excellence: Not a Passing Fancy But a Way of Life," which describes the rapid growth in the church he serves, Michael Schuler states why institutional excellence is so important to Unitarian Universalists committed to growth. "I have to believe that the success First Unitarian Society is enjoying has as much to do with the congregation's commitment to excellence as with the demographic trends that have seen millions of baby-boomers . . . drawn back to organized religion. . . . Being a boomer myself, I know that folks in my age cohort . . . aren't willing to settle for just *any* church. . . . Like me [they are] fairly discriminating; and they aren't really interested in a sloppy, slipshod operation. My peers don't accept mediocrity in their hospitals or in the schools their children attend. Why should they relax their standards when it comes to institutions that serve their spiritual needs?"

A congregation with a run-down building, poorly orchestrated worship, disorganized programming, and lackadaisical financial management will not attract members with high standards for their organizational affiliations. The excellence that attracts and holds new members, like growth itself, must be intentionally cultivated by both clergy and laity.

8. Encourage congregations to create institutional structures and habits that create high participation, high expectations, and high commitment.

Many, if not most, Unitarian Universalist congregations I have encountered in my twenty years in the ministry are places where membership, stewardship, and community service are taken quite casually. A low-participation, low-expectation, low-commitment church is likely to have low attendance figures, sparse programming, shabby buildings, lackluster outreach, and low member giving.

In her essay, "Responsibility and Commitment: Why Just 'Signing the Book' is Never Enough," Barbara Wells challenges "this norm of lightweight commitment to membership in Unitarian Universalist churches. In my experience casual commitment to membership translates into indifferent support for the church in all areas from volunteerism to financial support. Serious commitment . . . usually translates into real involvement at all levels. This kind of commitment and involvement eventually evolves into more active and engaging congregations. And active and engaging congregations attract people. . . . Growing churches are churches where high expectations and serious commitment are the norm."

Unitarian Universalists have tended to believe that high expectations for church members keep people away, the glorious mystery is that just *the opposite* is true—the more you expect, the more people want to affiliate with and serve this meaningful organization.

Getting Started

This book is designed for both ministerial and lay Unitarian Universalist leaders who are committed to Unitarian Universalist growth and extension. It is our hope that readers will be informed, excited, and inspired by this collection—to the end that they will be stimulated to action in their own congregations and UUA districts.

The twenty-two essays presented here are as diverse in style as they are in content. Written by a variety of Unitarian Universalist ministers, they represent a wide range of experience and perspective. But the unifying thread that runs through them all is devotion to the cause of Unitarian Universalism. Every contributor in this volume shares a commitment and a passion for the growth and health of our religious movement. These are truly "essays from the field," for every author is "out there in the vineyard" working to spread our "good news" and nurture UU congregations into the transformational and influential institu-

Introduction

tions they were meant to be.

Some of the essays present a historical view, and others describe what is just emerging today to shape our future. Some are vastly philosophical and others particularly practical. Some sketch broad strategies for growth and evangelism, and others focus on one factor necessary for such extension. Some of the essays address growth issues for Unitarian Universalist congregations in general, and others tell the specific story of one congregation and its particular strategies and experience. Taken together, they present a dynamic "big picture" of what is happening (and why) where Unitarian Universalism is growing and our message is being successfully shared.

This is *not* a complete and concise blueprint for growth and evangelism for *all* Unitarian Universalists, in *all* congregations, located in *all* communities. Rather, it is a smorgasbord feast, laid out for the reader to pick and choose those strategies, suggestions, and perspectives that are particularly palatable (and digestible). Like almost everything else in religious and church life, evangelism and growth don't suddenly or systematically happen overnight. They must arise *organically* and in phases (and even in fits and starts) in each unique setting—in ways appropriate to the variables that come into play and as available time, energy, and resources permit. What is important is *to get started*—to realize how terribly important it is for Unitarian Universalism to be shared more widely in your community and the world beyond, and then take intentional steps to help Unitarian Universalism grow where you live. In the end, it all comes down to the simple slogan of Nike's athletic shoe ads: *Just Do It!*

*Our History
and Tradition
of Evangelism*

Shout It Out, Folks:
We're Evangelists, Too!

John C. Morgan

A FEW WEEKS AGO, I happened to use "evangelism" in a sermon. As I was gathering together my notes and heading for the coffee, I noticed out of the corner of my eye that someone was marching toward me, face flushed, angry eyes looking for a landing spot on my psyche.

"Don't ever use that word here," she said.

"What word?" I asked innocently, already knowing from past experiences what she was going to say.

"Evangelism!" She drew back as if the word itself had caught in her throat. I think it had. "Don't use it again. We have newcomers here today!"

I wanted to ask how the newcomers had learned of this church if not from someone's evangelism, but I held my tongue. One learns in ministry that certain words trigger certain responses in our churches at certain times in our history (ten years ago, people had trouble with the word "God"). These days, the word evangelism seems to be whispered among those of us working in extension or growth ministries, but not yet openly voiced, and surely not on Sunday mornings, nor among people who still have a difficult time with words such as "worship" or "organization."

What a shame and what a loss for us! It's another case of a good word we have given over to those who heap abuse on it— the born-again television evangelists who, in the name of a wandering, poor Son of Man, raise funds to hire fundraisers to raise more funds.

I am not willing to keep quiet. I am an evangelist. It's in my family blood, it's in our spiritual blood, and without it our movement suffers a great loss of power and passion. I believe that spiritual communities grow by evangelism as fire grows by burning. If you light a match and then don't give it air, it will burn out. That has happened to a lot of our churches and fellowships that tried to hide our saving gospel and keep it to themselves. As a theological student some years ago, I was asked by the UUA Extension Department to take a look at 315 of our churches and fellowships that had died between 1961 and 1983. Again and again, in the records of these groups, I found a familiar refrain: inwardness, focusing on internal questions while neglecting a wider mission, with consequent loss of heart and mission. In short, I found no evangelism.

Conversely, if you light a fire and don't tend it, it can spread wildly and burn out of control. Fire needs nurturing. So, too, does evangelism. If we don't know what it is about ourselves which is worth sharing—know and feel the power of hundreds of years of Unitarian and Universalist history—then our evangelism will be rootless and even wither.

A simple definition of evangelism that makes sense to me as a Unitarian Universalist is this: Evangelism is sharing our dream with others in order to transform the world. Notice a few things about this definition.

1. *Evangelism is sharing.* It is not simply individualistic, although unless we feel the power of our dream personally, our sharing will seem shallow.

2. *Evangelism begins with a dream*, a vision that has power to claim some ultimate demand on our lives. Evangelism is not

about selling a commodity. Evangelism is about important issues, such as how to live and how to die, to what causes we are committed, and to whom we owe allegiance.

3. *Evangelism aims at transforming the whole world* to one bearing closer resemblance to our dream. Please note, some of us do not feel we can tell others what to believe. I don't believe in forcing our beliefs on others either, but I do believe the principles and purposes we express will make the world better. If I don't believe this, why bother? And if I can't share my faith with others, of what use is it?

4. *You have to understand and be committed to the dream in order to share it.* Sometimes, I suspect, the reason we don't share our faith is that we are a little embarrassed about how little we know of our own history, much less our own values. An effective evangelist is the bridge between the past and the future in the present moment. She or he knows the faith and, therefore, is not afraid to share it.

I am a relative newcomer to this mission of sharing our faith with others, yet in the past decade I have seen some of our congregations who wouldn't be caught alive with the word "evangelism" anywhere on their pamphlets, and some congregations for whom evangelism is the passion of their existence. I have seen some districts unable and/or unwilling to share their faith with others, and I know one district for which a primary reason for being is evangelism. I have seen some folks shift uncomfortably when the word evangelism is used and others, lately, relieved and even energized by the word. I have been a witness to some churches who can't and won't evangelize (and who are stuck), and others who evangelize as a normal part of their life (and who are growing).

Quite frankly, I am on the side of the evangelists. I have discovered, both in my own family history and most especially in the Universalist portion of our heritage, a rich and goodly evangelistic heritage: Evangelism is the power that has promoted our greatest periods of growth.

I believe that there is power and purpose in our Unitarian

Shout It Out, Folks

Universalist dream to shape the world around us into one more loving and just. I believe that a strong part of our heritage is evangelistic and that if our faith is deeply felt so, too, will it be shared with others naturally. I believe that the times are ripe for our saving message, because there are many people who would share our dream if we would let them know we are here. I believe that the key to our growth and vitality is evangelism, knowing and sharing our dream with others.

I bring two resources to bear upon the issue of evangelism for us as Unitarian Universalists. First, I bring my own family. I come from the "other side of the mountain," or the supposed other side of the argument. Both my grandfathers were evangelists, one known as one of the greatest of the early part of this century. Searching back through generations of circuit riders and nondenominational evangelists, I found in Vermont, on my mother's side, a Deist and radical, probably never acknowledged in my family trees. I cite these ancestors because much can be learned from them. After all, in spite of what we don't like about their theologies, we should give them credit for having the courage of their beliefs and an incredible record of new church starts, reaching new communities of people, and serving folks outside the mainstream (topics they not only discussed but also did something about).

Second, I bring a newcomer's understanding of how the early Universalists evangelized, and then, sometimes, failed to organize. I have come to appreciate not only the obvious early evangelists, such as John Murray, but also later ones, such as the Reverend George Rogers, called by some historians as "the second John Murray."

Finally, because I believe dreams must be incarnated and not just exist in some Platonic world of ideas, I want to highlight some of the remarkable developments in one project with which I was associated, the Northeast Pennsylvania Extension Project of the Joseph Priestley District. I find it very hopeful that in a part of the world where we had lost upwards of eleven churches, and where I was told nothing was possible because it was an area of the country too "working class" for us, we are growing again.

What My Family Heritage Has Taught Me

For too long, as is often true for other converts to Unitarian Universalism, my spiritual development was stuck in rebellion. I had a lot to rebel against: at least four generations of evangelists and preachers on my father's side and two on my mother's. I am not talking about polite, sit-back-and-wait-for-them-to-come-to-us missionaries—I'm talking about evangelists with a zest for missionary work. I'm talking about saving souls, pitching tents, riding circuits, and preaching the gospel in churches, fields, and homes.

For a long time I buried that part of my family tree, preferring instead to remember that ancestor who was a Vermont rebel, Deist, and radical. He, to my knowledge, died alone and unchurched.

I have finally come to the point in my life where I have been able to see the gifts of these evangelists, and, even, what we as modern-day liberals can learn from them. In some ways, they knew a great deal more about how to share the dream than we do, even with all our modern technologies. And while I do not share their theologies, I have come to appreciate their sense of mission.

By most accounts, G. Campbell Morgan was one of the great preachers of this century; he was also my grandfather. In evangelical circles, G. Campbell Morgan is known as the "prince of biblical expositors." By his own definition, however, my grandfather was first and foremost an evangelist. From his pulpit, he carried the dream of his Christian faith across continents, starting new churches, preaching to overflow crowds from Boston to London, giving weekday lectures to literally thousands gathered.

What can we learn about evangelism from one of its chief teachers? To answer this question, we can turn to a book that many Christian ministers still keep on their shelves: Morgan's classic, *The Ministry of the Word* (New York: Fleming H. Revell

Company, 1919), which is not only a theological treatise outlining the purpose and role of ministry, but also a practical book describing the practice of ministers.

Campbell Morgan grounds his understanding of ministry in the Christian tradition and, more directly, in the biblical record, beginning with the statement that ministry is the whole church, bound together by various gifts. Among the gifts of the church he includes those of apostles, prophets, evangelists, pastors, and teachers.

Apostles deal with the whole body of truth, stating it, making it available, and offering guidance. Prophets bring the truth to bear upon the life of the church and world. Pastors and teachers instruct others in how to live. This brings us to the purpose and role of the evangelist.

To evangelize is to proclaim good tidings. The important gift of the evangelist is that she or he feels the goodness of the news, knows it firsthand. Secondhand evangelism is not possible. The message is that of hope and love: "The evangelist then comes ever with joy and gladness. . . . A gloomy, pessimistic evangelist is a contradiction of terms. . . . The evangelist goes out in faith, in love, in hope" (*Ministry*, p. 101). The good news proclaimed is that of love, "as broad as the love of God, and as profound as humanity's deepest spiritual needs" (*Ministry*, p. 103).

What the evangelist requires is a response, a threefold claim: confidence, loyalty, cooperation. Confidence that the message does have ultimate meaning, loyalty to the cause being proclaimed, cooperation in its realization on earth.

Evangelism is always a cause or dream connected to an organization, in most cases, to a church. The whole purpose of evangelism is to bring others into the community of the dream, to convince others of the vision, to tell a compelling story and draw others into the circle. Evangelism, while personally rooted, is not individualistic, but profoundly relational. You cannot be an evangelist all by yourself.

Although separated from my grandfather theologically, I have found some of his understandings pertinent to us today;

let me cite a few lessons I have drawn.

1. We need to understand and feel in our hearts the "good news" we claim. This is the essential starting point, from which everything else flows. Without this, no growth programs will endure.

2. There are many gifts in our churches—in the old language, we still have apostles, teachers, pastors, and certainly prophets, but when and where do we nurture the role of evangelist in our congregations?

3. Evangelism requires a life response: confidence, loyalty, and cooperation. In a movement that for some time has not required cooperation as much as individualism, loyalty to a greater cause than personal growth is a hard lesson.

4. Evangelism is relational, not individualistic. The whole purpose of evangelism is to tell the good news so that others may share in its blessings. This, I believe, may be the major barrier for many Unitarian Universalists today: We think of evangelism, as we think of our mission as churches, in individualistic terms. We need to move from "me" to "us," from building communities only to support "individual freedom of belief" to building communities of shared memories and powerful common dreams. And we need to be bold enough to dream, and not just wish, that the whole world would be a much better place if our deepest values were adopted by more than a handful of folks in North America.

Reconnecting With Our Universalist Heritage

In the past eight years, I learned about Universalist evangelists that make some of my ancestors look tame by comparison. Most of us know John Murray's story of coming to America and finding Thomas Potter's chapel in the New Jersey woods. Murray arrived there in 1770; the chapel was built in 1760. Has anyone thought to ask just what was a chapel built for a Universalist minister doing in the woods in 1760? And why did an illiterate, Quaker/Universalist like Thomas Potter build such a chapel? Though, we don't know the full story, it was probably because evangelists preached Universalism in Potter's part of the world long before John Murray arrived (we do know, for example, that preachers from the Ephrata Cloister in Pennsylvania were preaching Universalism long before Universalists).

Many of us also have heard about Quillen Shinn, the great evangelist and builder of new Universalist churches. But how many of us know that one of the earliest preachers of Universalism, Dr. George de Benneville of Pennsylvania, considered himself an evangelist/missionary, carrying our gospel south and west in the eighteenth century? Do we remember Maria Cook, an early circuit rider? How many of us realize that the radical evangelistic impulse of Revolutionary New England was fueled by Universalists, among others? Do we remember, for example, the names of Caleb Rich, Isaac Davis, or Adam Streeter—Universalist evangelists all?

One early Universalist evangelist and circuit rider, the Reverend George Rogers, provides an excellent example of how some of these early Universalist evangelists worked. I also have drawn insights from a book that should be read by anyone wishing to come to terms with our evangelical roots, *Radical Sects of Revolutionary New England* by Stephen A. Marini (Cambridge, MA: Harvard University Press, 1982). Marini describes the pattern of early Universalist evangelism (which I have adapted here) and the reasons why Universalists could evangelize but not always grow (minimal organization and maximum individualism are two major reasons, both of which, I suspect, are still with us today in some degree).

In studying the patterns of evangelism—sharing the good news of the Universalist gospel with others—it became clear to me that a system was at work. Although particular aspects of the system varied greatly by area and by evangelist, all the methods were geared toward extending the Universalist faith to new communities of people, often by a charismatic figure under direct marching orders from the Almighty. If the Unitarian movement was the liberalization of the established order of the Boston environs, then it might well be said the Universalist movement in that part of New England outside Boston was the enthusiastic rejection of the established order and the creation of a revivalistic, evangelistic, spirit-filled network of fiercely independent communities of people.

The evangelistic pattern of Universalists, at least as portrayed by Marini and seen in the missionary ventures of George Rogers, seemed to follow the following kind of outreach:

1. Itinerant preaching on a more or less hit-or-miss basis by a Universalist circuit rider with the hope of reaching as many isolated people as possible.

2. Over time, a series of informal preaching stations would be established by a visiting preacher, where over a "circuit," the preacher would travel throughout the year.

3. As time went by, small, informal networks of people would gather, often in small towns and many times among families. Sometimes, people would meet in each other's homes, other times a courthouse or meeting house could be secured, often against the protests of the more established faiths.

4. Evangelists might speak in churches, sometimes in ones already called Universalist and other times in those of other religious traditions. It was not unheard of that a segment of another tradition, having heard the Universalist message, might break off and form a separate congregation.

5. Finally, as the movement grew, evangelism reached beyond individual communities or churches into more regional bodies, such as conventions. These are early examples of more regionalized Universalist attempts at sharing the faith; the groups meeting appeared to restate their commitment to congregational polity and suspicion of wider associations.

The Reverend George Rogers (1804-1846), was an intriguing, often humorous Universalist evangelist who spread Universalist ideas and institutions far and wide. During his ministry, Rogers preached in almost all the states of the union and ventured into parts of Canada as well. His *Memoranda of the Experience, Labors and Travels of a Universalist Preacher,*

Shout It Out, Folks

Written by Himself (Cincinnati, OH: John A. Gurley, 1845) is an intriguing story of an early Universalist evangelist. This book ought to be reissued and read by everyone concerned with sharing our faith.

George Rogers was an orphan, arriving in this country from England in 1818. He spent his early years in a Philadelphia orphanage, an experience he said contributed to his desire to be on the open road. He loved to read, wrote poems, and moved from one religious group to another in his early years.

Initially strongly opposed to Universalism, Rogers became convinced of its truths. He once gave a sermon on the trinity in a Presbyterian church, and by the end of his discourse he had adopted a Unitarian view! Moreover, he had become a Universalist as well, believing that God's goodness was inherent. He preached independently for a while and delivered his first sermon to Universalists in Philadelphia. In the spring of 1831, he became pastor of a Universalist church in Brooklyn, Pennsylvania. He was never to settle anywhere for a long time, however; his pastorates were frequently springing-off points for evangelism.

It is to his first evangelistic journey that I turn as a way of illustrating how these early circuit riders functioned.

In December, 1834, Rogers began a missionary trip to the "West" (Ohio). His mode of travel was horseback, and he recounts stories of snow and dangers throughout. In the first part of his trip, he preached wherever he could: Easton, Reading, Bethlehem, Wommelsdorf (where he spoke in English to a German congregation), Pottsville, and Reamstown. Finally, he preached at a German Lutheran Church in Lancaster, where a mob rushed the place, attacking the vestryman and attempting "to strangle the sexton" (*Memoranda*, p. 147). This meeting was canceled, and Rogers continued to Harrisburg, then a city of 4,000, where he preached in the Unitarian church, "not to large congregations, for it is a place of no small amount of bigotry" (*Memoranda*, p. 147). Rogers did note, however, that in Harrisburg many of the Lutheran pastors tended to hold Universalist views privately.

In Pittsburgh, Rogers sought out friends and spoke at the courthouse in spite of local opposition, believing himself to be the first Universalist preacher to do so. Local clergy arrived to protest his visit; rocks were thrown through the windows, and some were broken. Rogers informed those gathered that their behavior gave evidence against the religion they purported to believe. "Let me tell you, my friends," he said, "you have mistaken your man; I am not thus to be stopped: I would preach the love of God at the martyr's stake" (*Memoranda*, p. 153). Soon, 200 people came to another meeting.

Rogers continued his journey to Wheeling, West Virginia, then to Zanesville, Ohio, where he preached nine times. Then, he spent four days in Marietta, a few in Belpre, where he preached in a Universalist building, and finally went to Cincinnati. He stayed there for two weeks, delivering seventeen sermons, one in a Unitarian church. He writes of this visit: "The friends call it a revival, and so it was; for why may not truth be revived as well as fanaticism?" (*Memoranda*, p. 157). Before leaving, Rogers had organized the core of a revived church, promising to return to them as their pastor.

From Cincinnati, Rogers headed back to Pennsylvania, but by a different route so he could do more evangelizing! He traveled through Chillicothe, Lancaster, Newark, Mount Vernon, and Mansfield (where he delivered two sermons). He performed a marriage ceremony in Mansfield, but an arrest warrant was issued because he was not licensed to do so. He then went to Peru and also to Huron, where he took passage on a steamboat for Buffalo. He writes: "I had now traveled over Ohio in zigzag directions, for four hundred miles. . . . I became seized with a burning desire it should become . . . a field of Universalist labor" (*Memoranda*, p. 160). How disappointed he would be to hear today that where there once had been well over a hundred Universalist churches in Ohio alone, there are now only about forty-five Unitarian Universalist churches in a district that includes most of Ohio, West Virginia, and the western part of Pennsylvania.

Shout It Out, Folks

Rogers' evangelistic style, and that of others, illustrates a number of important lessons for us today. First, and most obvious, there was a heartfelt, saving message these circuit riders had to share. In a day when we hesitate to travel more than twenty minutes to church, their commitment puts us to shame. Second, the style worked to spread the good news and provide visibility. It was controversial in nature, but it shared our gospel with others wherever it might be heard. Third, it was dependent on a charismatic figure. And fourth, it emphasized personal evangelism, leading to a change of heart and behavior.

There are a few evangelistic approaches we ought not repeat, as well. The first is that although the approaches were broad, they were not well planned in terms of continuing to nurture the seeds planted. Future organizational developments were minimized; hence, strong churches might not arise out of the seed planted. Second, the approach was personal, but also individualistic. Out of such individualism, how might community be nurtured?

Incarnating Our Faith in New Communities of People

As my grandfather often wrote, personal evangelism is needed to convince the heart, but evangelism apart from the church tends not to mature. The lessons of our Universalist evangelists might be that we need to heed their cry for sharing our faith with others, but become wiser about how we plant the seeds of organization.

The planting image of evangelism is a good one, for essentially it requires the seed (the message or vision), the planter (the evangelist), and the gardener (the one who helps the seed to grow by nurturing it). Without the seed, the vision, nothing will finally grow. Without someone to plant the seed, nothing grows from it. And without someone to nurture the growth, the seed dies.

I believe that we as Unitarian Universalists have often adapted evangelism to fit our prevailing organizational culture. Hence, we have done more with printed brochures and media outreach, because this matches the predominantly verbal and educational bias of our movement. And, even when it comes to advertising, my suspicion is that we advertise to attract those we think will be "like us," and avoid advertising that might speak to new audiences. If we can advertise over a classical radio station, why not one with soul music or rock?

I also believe that given the emphasis we have placed on individualism, it has been difficult for us to refocus on evangelism as a organizational issue. Hence, we have not done as much as we should to start new, strong congregations, a strategy most other denominations realize is the single most effective approach to overall church growth and to diversification. Fundamentally, I believe, our evangelistic mission is not simply to take our message to the airways, but, more importantly, to put our bodies where our message tells us to put them, which, I believe, has something to do with starting new congregations that are not just suburban, relatively wealthy, mostly professional, and white.

For the past ten years of my ministry, I have sought to be an evangelist for our cause by trying to make our presence known in new communities of people. Along the way, I have heard the arguments against what I am proposing; let me repeat a few.

1. "Go with our strengths." This argument fundamentally states that our "strengths" are in organizing folks who are predominantly white, mostly suburban, and clearly among the most educated and highest income of Americans.

2. Our message only appeals to a small handful of folks who are broad and searching enough to grasp its subtle messages.

3. Ours is predominantly a rationalistic faith that will deny itself if it borders on emotionalism, evangelism, or missionary work.

4. Smallness is what we are about, and "big churches" somehow are contrary to our purposes (as are, I would add, "big denominations").

5. We're just too diverse to grow. Growing movements have a clear message, a degree of centralized authority, and a cadre of "true believers."

All of the above arguments contain elements of truth. We

have become a denomination that has a larger percentage of higher educated and income people. Thanks to the fellowship movement, we also have tended in the past to start smaller new groups (it used to be that it took only ten persons to start a fellowship). Many members saw these groups as alternatives to what they perceived as large, impersonal churches. And, we have tended to be a verbal religion, one a little suspicious of uncontrollable emotions. And, finally, we have lauded pluralism but have been unclear about the parameters of our pluralism and a little soft around the center.

I would argue that these arguments may be descriptive, but not proscriptive. That is, they may give us some clues about where we have recently been, but not necessarily tell us where we ought to be going. Neither do they define our potential.

Every reformation begins with a small step. I think that is what is happening among us now. I can see the seeds of the reformation planted in the early work of the UUA Extension Department, where people like Joan Goodwin, Bill Holway, Tom Chulak, Lucy Hitchcock, and Mel Hoover wrestled mightily with how to extend our faith into new communities of people. I also have had the incredible fortune to be the first extension minister for a district (Joseph Priestley District) that defined its mission as sharing the faith. Maybe this explains why it is the largest district in the UUA. A sense of mission has pervaded this work. Arguments have risen over strategies, but not once do I recall a disagreement over sharing our faith with others. The vision was good, the need clear, and the leadership committed.

In 1989, I remember meeting with some district folks about the northeast sector of Pennsylvania. The district was growing by leaps and bounds elsewhere, but not in the northeast: In the past two decades, we had lost eleven of our churches or fellowships there. Some thought it was an economically disadvantaged region, certainly not one fitting the stereotypes of where our potential might be greatest. Nevertheless, rather than wringing its hands, the district decided to be proactive and start a three-year project in northeastern Pennsylvania, supported by monies from both the Fund for Unitarian Universalism and the Pennsylvania Universalist Convention.

Not all our efforts were effective in three years; we are sometimes naive in our evangelism. Other denominations plan long range, invest early on, and stay in for a decade. We were fortunate to have three years in northeastern Pennsylvania. Two new congregations are still struggling, and three are relatively healthy. They are all more or less economically diverse. One of these is housed in the restored Joseph Priestley Chapel in Northumberland, Pennsylvania. A series of other activities rippled as a result of the evangelism, including new persons considering the UU ministry, and other area churches organizing to help. In an early headline from a local newspaper near Northumberland, the headline read: "Unitarian Revival Underway. . . ." In the final home of Dr. Joseph Priestley, perhaps one might forgive the headline writer's omission of Universalism, but what pleased me was that the Joseph Priestley District board was delighted by the word, "revival," feeling that it expressed their mission!

As I have reflected on why I believe this project worked to a great extent, embodying what I believe is the essential mission of evangelism—to create new communities of people—a few important lessons can be learned.

1. Start with a clear sense of identity and mission. If you don't know who you are, how can you share the faith? And, if you don't know where you are going, you're likely to end up there.

2. From the very beginning, seek out and nurture committed leadership, share gifts, avoid blame, and inspire others.

3. Organize, don't mourn, and follow through, don't fall through.

4. Do a few things well. Have a high quality of worship and religious education for adults and children.

5. Don't just serve yourselves, but remind yourselves of the communities in which you live and the wider movement of which you are a part.

6. Play and work together. Don't take everything seriously.

Shout It Out, Folks

Learn how to play. Express warmth and enthusiasm. Say thank you. And, sometimes, say no to people.

7. Create many small groups to meet a variety of needs.

8. Realize that evangelism is what the church does when it feels it has a saving message and cannot help but share it with the world. Don't limit yourself. Be a community of the spirit.

Conclusion

I do believe we have a saving vision that the world needs to hear and see. It needs to hear what we say, but also see that we live the values we profess in our life together. In the long run, it will do us very little good to profess one thing with our mouths and deny the same thing in our actions. The best vehicle for evangelism is truly believing in our own vision, and then living that vision among ourselves and in the wider world.

Evangelism, especially in our tradition, also needs to renew its corporate focus. Obviously, to be effective, evangelism needs to be personal. Each one of us needs to be clear in our minds and hearts of our spiritual convictions and be willing to share those convictions with others. Nevertheless, without intentionally creating evangelistic organizations, our personal strategies will not find community support. What if, for example, we saw the need for new Unitarian Universalist "mission outposts" as expressions of our evangelism? What if we renewed our extension into the inner cities, into predominantly working class towns and cities, into areas left unattended by us? What if, like so many other denominations, we actually moved to add a new ministerial category to our classifications other than parish or community, calling this one "evangelist ministry"?

We have such a deep and rich heritage. We have a vision to share. And we have just begun again. Might we not one day say, as the Reverend George Rogers said in 1844, "The friends call it a revival; and so it was; for why may not truth be revived as well as fanaticism?"

Why not, indeed!

Answering the Religious Right with the Big Heart of Universalism

Scott W. Alexander

THESE ARE TIMES OF great tension and conflict in our culture. Much of this turmoil in the United States is focused on what many observers have called "The Culture Wars," the very vocal and visible battles that are occurring on many fronts to determine whose values, principles, beliefs, and perspectives will determine the shape of public and private life. In particular, over the last several years, religious and cultural conservatives are waging a fierce battle against what they perceive to be the evils of liberalism—including the availability of abortion and sex education; the affirmation and protection of gay, lesbian, and bisexual persons; and the cultural inclusion of minorities and women by means of multiculturalism and feminism. Radical reactionary Christians and other conservatives are passionately convinced that there has been a dangerous erosion of the old standards of American life, a dangerous shift away from the assumptions and ideas that *they believe* built and sustained our nation. At a recent meeting of an American group called the Christian Coalition, Pat Buchanan repeated his oft-heard battle cry, "We are in a war for the soul of the American people."

Answering the Religious Right

I'm afraid Pat Buchanan is right. Like it or not a war *is* now being waged in our culture: The intellectual and spiritual battle lines have been drawn, and a very important struggle is under way between competing ideas and values—between competing visions of what our society is going to look and feel like in the next century. I believe it is crucial that we Unitarian Universalists *not* sit on the sidelines of these culture wars. As religious people with a good and decent vision for human persons and society, we must speak up and stand up for our values and beliefs—speak up and stand up for the principles that give our religion its large heart and enduring beauty.

The cultural and religious struggle we are now in may seem new but nothing could be further from the truth. In fact Universalism, the 200-year-old faith upon which this church was built, arose in just such a time of deep societal conflict.

As we struggle to gain perspective on these conflicted times and how we as religious people should respond, let us begin back at the beginning. American Universalism, like its spiritual sister American Unitarianism, began as a radical and optimistic Christian heresy in response to the grim doctrines of eighteenth-century Calvinistic Puritanism. The story of how and why Universalism took root can perhaps be told most clearly by contrasting the messages of two of the greatest preachers of that day, Jonathan Edwards and Hosea Ballou.

Jonathan Edwards was a puritan's puritan, the most renowned preacher of what was called "The Great Awakening," an early version of a born-again Christian fundamentalist revival that occurred in the late 1700s. He was an athletic and charismatic man who had the power (and predilection) during his preaching to bring whole congregations to fearful wailing as he described the misery and damnation that they both deserved—and would receive in hell—at the hands of an angry God. Sometimes in the pulpit he would rip off his robes and tear his linen shirt to shreds in self-abasing frenzy and disgust. Consider a portion of one of his more famous sermons in which he tells the listeners that they are "sinners in the hands of an angry God."

The world of misery, the lake of burning brimstone, is extended abroad under you. . . . Hell's gaping mouth [is] wide open, and you have nothing to stand upon or take hold of. . . . It is only the power and mere pleasure of God that holds you up. . . . The God that holds you over the pit of hell, much as one holds a spider or some loathsome insect over the fire, abhors you. You have offended him . . . O Sinner! You hang by a slender thread, with the flames of divine wrath flashing about it, and ready every moment to singe . . . and burn it asunder. You have nothing to lay hold of to save yourself. There is nothing that you have ever done, nothing that you can do, to induce God to spare you one moment.

On another happy occasion, Edwards told the brow-beaten folks in the pews that whenever God catches the scent of humanity, the human smell is so foul and putrid it causes God to "flair his nostrils in disgust!" Cheerful stuff, this eighteenth-century Puritanism! But this was the substance and soul of the predominating Calvinistic theology of the day: God is a distant, angry, and stern judge; humanity is a fallen and sinful beast; and most men, women, and children are doomed to a hell of eternal damnation and misery for all their weakness and wickedness.

It was over this dark and forbidding spiritual landscape that the fresh and warm breezes of Universalism blew—a theology of love, reconciliation, and hope. The early Universalists, in direct spiritual contradiction to Puritanism's gloomy gospel, simply proclaimed that the essential qualities of God were not wrath, disgust, and judgment but goodness, mercy, and love. The heart-felt good news of Universalism was that by God's grace and power all of God's children (every man, woman, and child—regardless of station or personality, weakness, or wickedness) would ultimately be saved, welcomed back by an embracing and understanding creator. God's salvation was offered to all, to the end that (as one early Universalist put it) "the last sinner will be dragged kicking and cursing into heaven." Universalist preachers proclaimed every human being to be a child of God—quite naturally possessing their divine parent's inclination toward goodness and right, and therefore unavoidably drawn toward heaven and health by God's all-powerful and encompassing love. Universalism's life blood was the spiritual insistence that the evil and pain we see in our world need not be a permanent and pervasive part of the human condition. The early Universalists dreamed a larger hope than sin-saturated Puritanism and passionately believed that the natural inclination of God, humanity, indeed creation itself is toward the good. The American people (hungry for positive, hopeful, people-oriented religion) flocked to Universalist churches—at one time in the 1840s Universalism was the sixth largest American denomination.

The greatest Universalist theologian and preacher of the day was the Reverend Hosea Ballou. Every bit the orator of his "Great Awakening" adversaries, Ballou used to hold his large congregations spellbound as he gently and joyfully proclaimed this gospel of universal salvation. Once, before a huge congregation in Philadelphia, he pointed to the children in his audience and expressed his horror that many of the parents present that day held to the prevailing Calvinist assertion that their children were innately depraved, and that most were already doomed to eternal damnation. Lifting his hand from the Bible and pointing over the crowd he cried, "O dear man! Dear woman! Have you no connections in the world? Are you insulated from human nature? I ask you to look at the companion of your bosom . . . look on the child of your love, and say if you believe it probable that these connections were originally doomed by the decree of heaven to everlasting wretchedness, and derive consolation from that belief?"

Once, when another Universalist evangelist, John Murray, was preaching in Boston, a rock sailed through the window and landed near him (remember, even back then there was a battle going on for the soul of this culture). Without missing a beat, he picked up the large stone and said, "This argument is solid and weighty, but it is neither reasonable nor convincing." Then putting the rock aside, he added, "Not all the stones in Boston, lest they stop my breath, shall shut my mouth." The early American Universalists bravely preached a gospel of inclusion, reconciliation, and hope right in the face of Calvinistic negativity. Theirs was a gospel that unashamedly affirmed the oneness and worth of all persons.

When I first studied eighteenth- and nineteenth-century Universalist thought during my years in seminary, I was profoundly taken by this bold and positive faith position. What captured my spiritual attention was the large and embracing spirit of Universalism; the big and beautiful heart of Universalism; the deep and compassionate conviction our Universalist forebears had in the basic, deep-down, unquenchable goodness of creation, human society, and persons.

In those days I went as far as describing myself as a Universalist Unitarian, not only because I was raised in a Universalist church, but also by way of affirming my interest in and allegiance to the Universalist principles of inclusion, optimism, compassion, and hope. During my final year in seminary, I decided to do a chapel for the faculty and students at the school, at which time I planned to expound on this pure and lovely gospel of universal human affirmation.

The morning of the chapel, I arose early and poured over my powerful and polemically perfect text. I was privately proud in advance of the depth and passion with which I grasped the essence of my Universalist heritage. As I walked the mile or so from my home to the school, my head was down as I silently rehearsed to myself all of the beautiful phrases I had crafted to make my sermon on Universalism come alive. As I approached a busy intersection, I happened to glance up and see an incredibly large woman sitting on a bench waiting for the bus. Now, I have always had a personal obsession about my own weight, and in those years was quite prejudiced and opinionated about people who weighed more than I thought they should. Before I could censor the unkind, judgmental thought, I blurted out to myself, "Oh, dear God look at that gross woman. She must weigh 400 pounds. How could anyone ever let themselves get like that and who could ever love that?"

And at that moment, as if it were a bolt of spiritual lightning aimed right at me, a skinny little guy sitting next to her looked lovingly into her eyes, leaned over, and gave her the most gentle and loving kiss I have ever seen one human being bestow upon another. I was stunned and ashamed. And while I was still reeling from the jarring disparity between my petty and unkind judgment and his pure and simple love, a voice (without words, but in unmistakable clarity, holiness, and power) . . . a voice came out of the whirlwind and said to me (and to me alone) "Don't you get it, you dope? Here you are, at this very moment going up the hill to preach your clever little sermon on God's love and universal salvation for every human person, and all you can do is sneer inside at someone you deem unworthy and unbeautiful. Don't you understand that, in the eyes of all that is sacred and beautiful and holy and true in this creation, she is as utterly lovely as human beings get? Don't you get it? If the pleasures and prerogatives, graces and goddesses of this creation are made for you (and you certainly claim them as a natural birthright for yourself) then they are made for her, too. And you call yourself a Universalist . . . puffff."

I was as startled as I was chastened. In that moment of pure and precious spiritual revelation, a spirit of holiness I can only call God spoke to me with heart-numbing clarity, and I finally began to understand Universalism viscerally, deep in my bones. What it means to be a Universalist, a real Universalist in more than name only, is to have a heart that seeks and sees at every human turn the natural worth and preciousness of people—all people—especially those very different from oneself. In an instant, I understood what a wild and welcoming a doctrine our Universalist forebears bequeathed to us, and that doctrine can be summed up in stark simplicity: There is a place set in this creation for every last man, woman, and child. A precious, safe place has been set for each and every one of us—period! And it is our human job to respect, protect, and nurture the well-being of all of God's diverse and curious children. The early Universalists said, pure and simple, that every human being, no matter how strange or flawed or unlovable or broken or weird they may seem, is to be protected, cherished, welcomed, loved.

This is not an easy faith to have in these waning years of the twentieth century. Our time, I need not point out, has so much human violence, cruelty, and degradation. A look into the daily newspapers provides the evidence—genocide in Bosnia, war lords in Somalia, senseless and serial killers all across North America—the manifestations of our human depravity are nearly endless. This is not an easy time to believe in the worth and redeemability of all persons and every society.

But Universalism, Universalism then and now, is not a naive and foolish faith, one that cannot see human wickedness, foible, and sin. Rather, it is a tenacious faith. Universalism is a promise to theologically hang in there with the complexities and cruelties of the human enterprise. It is the promise not to give up on people, but to keep struggling in our broken world for the inclusion of all—even those one might naturally want to despise, reject, condemn, or judge. They simply refused to give up on people. They saw the oneness and worth of humanity more than our separateness and sin.

But many in our culture have a far different theology of persons. Just as in 1793 (when the Puritans and Universalists were theologically battling it out in the public square for the hearts and minds of the people) once again today there is struggle, a very real struggle, over the soul of our nation. Today, the radical religious right (who are fervently vocal, fiercely organized, and frightfully well funded) are preaching the same negative and judgmental human message that Jonathan Edwards preached 200 years ago. The theological and social message of the religious right is the exact opposite of Universalism's tenacious acceptance of every human person. Persons like Pat Robertson and Jerry Falwell see God as angry and punishing and believe humanity must be divided, ripped asunder, "sheep from goats," "saints from sinners." They are not the least bit shy about declaring that righteous delineations must be drawn between the "saved" and the "damned," between the "right-thinking" and the "wrong," between the "pure" and the "defiled," between God's chosen "religiously correct" (for whom a place has been set) and the devil's legions (all those others for whom a place at creation's table has—in their worldview—*not* been set!

Pat Robertson and Pat Buchanan and other neopuritanical spokespersons have declared a holy war, a righteous *jihad*, against all who have different lifestyles, beliefs, values, worldviews, and even social and political philosophies. And these vocal new Puritans (who number in the many millions) are not satisfied with swaying individuals to their worldview, the radical religious right demands that society and government be structured in ways that reflect their narrow perspectives, and their narrow perspectives only.

We ignore these latter-day clones of Jonathan Edwards and their angry, narrow, and hateful religious vision at our own peril. I believe with all my heart and soul that in this dangerous time of culture wars we must *answer* the religious right. We must answer them, pure and simple, with the truth that is Universalism.

Does that seem too bold a statement? Does it seem too dogmatic or opinionated? I'm sorry, but I see no room for equivocation here. Universalism, that big-hearted faith that sees the oneness and wonderfulness of all people everywhere, even in all their diversity and difficulty, is good and true. It is a sound and saving vision for the human family that can help us create a livable world for all. That is why we must not hide the light of our faith under some bushel of meek and mild politeness while the Jerry Falwells of this world preach their divisive, fearful, exclusionary message to millions. We must boldly and unashamedly share our "good news" that every man, woman, and child of this creation—be they young or old, black or white, rich or poor, yellow or brown, liberal or conservative, gay or straight—is a child of God, a valuable creature fashioned out of high and holy stuff, for whom a place at life's table has been set. Wherever we are, however we find ourselves stationed in life, we must share that faith, tell that truth, live that ethic, dare that dream. John Murray, the man who is credited with bringing Universalism to America, put it this way, "You possess only a small light, but uncover it, let it shine, use it in order to bring more light and understanding to the hearts and minds of men and women. Give them not hell, but hope and courage."

We must unashamedly stand up in this culture and, without arrogance or vitriol, even with an appreciation for the integrity and thoughtfulness of many evangelical Christians, give voice to our theological beliefs and spiritual perspectives just like our optimistic and unashamed Universalist forebears did. We must be the brave and forthright messengers of their larger hope for the whole of the human family. We must not sit back complacently, in that self-satisfied smugness that is so common in "right-thinking" religious liberals and let their centuries-old vision for a better, kinder world die because of our sophisticated cowardice or neglect. We must speak and live and share the generous heart of Universalism.

The bottom line is that, like it or not, we must be *evangelists*, unashamed evangelists willing to speak up for the kind and generous truth that is Universalism. The word "evangelist" carries extremely negative connotations for many of us. Most Unitarian Universalists probably think of evangelists as pushy, arrogant, obnoxious zealots who sell religion on television or door-to-door, because that does accurately describe many conservative Christian evangelists we have had the misfortune of encountering over the years. But is it possible that the only reason we think so poorly of evangelists is that next to nobody who thinks or feels as we do religiously ever engages in the process of publicly sharing their faith? Unitarian Universalists are notoriously spiritually silent. Because we demand to think for ourselves, are respectful of human difference, and don't appreciate it when someone else tries to ram their beliefs down our throats, we tend to shy away from even cautiously and respectfully sharing with others what it is we believe, and how those beliefs help us strive to be better, kinder, larger people. It is hard for some of us to talk back to fundamentalism by "talking up" our own faith, but I passionately believe we cannot afford such a self-imposed silence in dangerous and divisive times such as these.

We can wish it all we want, but the proselytizing and political action of the religious right are not going to just fade away. The proponents of these beliefs are out there in the public square, on the public airwaves. They are running "stealth" candidates in local elections and trying to take over school and library boards, town and county offices, even national party structures in many states. Unless other, gentler visions for the human family are given voice, this divisive message will be the only one heard. If we remove ourselves from the religious playing field (by being too polite or nonconfrontational to say what it is we believe and why we believe it and strive to live in accordance with it) then other messages will carry the day, and neither we nor humanity can afford that. So let us be kind, gentle, respectful evangelists for that hopeful, inclusive human vision bequeathed to us by our Universalist forbears. The stakes are too high for anything less.

It is not enough simply to speak up about Universalism with our lips. We must further speak it with our lives, with the deeds and doings of our hands and hearts. And let there be no illusions about it, Universalism is a tough and radical doctrine. It is a hard and demanding gospel, for it insists that we each be constantly growing bigger, more inclusive and caring hearts, setting aside our little fears and prejudices as we strive to care ever more widely for our brothers and sisters in the world. The demanding call of Universalism is a tough and foolish doctrine of inclusion and care that constantly challenges us beyond the narrow confines of our natural selfishness and fear to ever wider circles of caring and compassion.

I pray that in the days and years ahead, we who call ourselves Unitarian Universalists will speak the generous, inclusive, affirming spirit of Universalism with our lips as we answer those who live by meaner and more divisive doctrines, and, even more challenging, speak it with our lives. Speak it until everyone across this great and troubled land begins to hear on the wind the holy and inclusive voice that says we are all God's children.

Bring Them Hope, Not Hell

*A Short History of
Universalist and
Unitarian Evangelism*

Carl G. Seaburg

UNIVERSALISM BEGAN AS an evangelistic movement. It had a mission, bringing a liberating concept (that God would save all humans) to a dried-up Calvinism that held to a stern belief that most of humanity had been doomed to everlasting hell before they were even born. All the early Universalists—Murray, Winchester, Ballou—operated as evangelists. They came into communities and promoted this new doctrine, the doctrine of universal salvation. They denounced the reigning doctrine of election, predestination, and eternal damnation by a vindictive judging God. From the first, Universalists *had* to be evangelists; they were bearers of "good news" to troubled people.

Certainly their sermons were evangelistic in nature because many of their auditors were not Universalist but came to hear this strange doctrine preached to see if they agreed with it or not. One Sunday evening in July 1819, a young bootmaker's apprentice going home walked by the Second Universalist Society on School Street in Boston. Seeing it lit up, curiosity led him to go in and listen to Hosea Ballou's sermon on the love of God. He started attending, volunteered to play the cello in the church choir, and by the fall of 1820 he began studying for the ministry under Ballou. Thomas Whittemore went on to a distinguished career as a Universalist preacher and editor.

Universalist ministers were also constantly challenged about their beliefs. Murray's and Ballou's biographies are full of such educational opportunities, as the following anecdote about Hosea Ballou shows.

In 1799 he came to Reading, Vermont, to preach and was confronted before the service by a deacon from the Baptist Church, who wanted to ask him a question.

"Are you," said he, "the Mr. Ballou who is to preach here this afternoon?"

"I am," replied Mr. Ballou.

"Well, Mr. Ballou, I understand you are in a great hurry, but I must take time to ask you one question. Mr. Ballou, what do you think of the case of a man who should go out of the world cursing and swearing, and calling on God to damn his soul?"

Mr. Ballou had but a moment that he could devote to the man, and he said, "Why, deacon, a profane swearer is a very, very wicked man, no doubt; and do you think God *will* answer the prayer of so wicked a man as that?"

"No," said the deacon, "I am *sure* he will not."

"Well, deacon," said Mr. Ballou, "you have answered your own question," and he passed into the house where the people were waiting for service to begin.

The Universalists were active in spreading their version of the gospel. They felt they had truly "good news" to bring to people disturbed that they or their innocent children might spend an eternity in hell.

Although Universalism was associated historically with New England, as people migrated westward, the preachers went with them. "Circuit riders" they were called, not serving one settled parish, but traveling on horseback and preaching the gospel in all the new settlements.

Baptists and Methodists were most active in providing circuit riders to these emigrants. The Unitarians made almost no effort for many years to reach out to these new communities. The Universalists, however, were much more adventuresome. Sydney Ahlstrom has observed that Universalists were "far more evangelical than is generally realized. . . . On the frontier their views frequently found favor."

While Methodists and Baptists held camp meetings, often spread over many days, the Universalists generally went in for public debates. The circuit riders were ordinarily young, usually had little more than a grammar school education, more likely had come from a rural area rather than a city, and preferred to travel rather than settle down. Give him a good horse, a sturdy pair of boots, and the hospitality of strangers, and he was off into the wilderness bringing the good news of universal salvation.

Usually they found themselves to be the first Universalist some of these people had ever heard or met. They had to fend for themselves with no backing, financially or otherwise, from central or regional headquarters. But there were a surprising number of such men in the field spreading the Universalist gospel. For instance, even before Iowa became a territory in the late 1830s, more than thirty circuit riders were plowing that field. The Reverend T. C. Eaton was in the state for some fourteen months and recorded in his diary that he had traveled in twelve counties covering 9,000 miles. As he broke it down, 3,000 miles had been on horseback, 2,000 in buggies, and 4,000 on the railroad.

Many of these circuit riders were obscure, and quite a few of their names are lost to history. One of the more noted ones was Nathaniel Stacy, who in spite of poor health brought the good news of Universalism to much of New York and Pennsylvania. Another was George Rogers, small with a high-pitched voice, a sturdy constitution, and a well-developed sense of humor, who, in the 1830s and 1840s, brought the Universalist message to the Southern states and the border states of the Midwest. He preached in theaters, in barns, in forest clearings, in private homes, in Universalist churches where he could find them, and in churches of other denominations if they let him in. He rarely rested.

In Tennessee on one of his trips, he preached nineteen sermons in sixteen days. And these were not twenty-minute sermons either! One of his last trips stretched from St. Louis to Burlington, Iowa, and back to Massachusetts, New Hampshire, and Maine. He died in 1846 of tuberculosis at the age of 42. Abel Thomas called him "the most active, persevering, widely-operating missionary ever connected with our denomination."

Some of the churches these circuit riders started never went anywhere. They were built at the crossing of two roads, with only a few people in the neighborhood. Too many were in remote rural areas and never prospered. Others went on to become well established and survive to this day. But no one can question either the determination, perseverance, and dedication of these traveling missionaries or their desire to bring word of the larger hope to as many people as they could reach.

The Universalists were also well aware of the power of the press. They published some 182 periodicals in these early years, including weekly, monthly, and quarterly newspapers. Subscribers ranged from a few hundred for some of these papers to up to 5,000 for the principal ones. In addition there were Sunday school papers. The heyday of such publications was between 1820 and 1850, which, historian Russell Miller points out, coincided with a period of significant denominational growth. "In that period, books and pamphlets appeared at the rate of over thirty a year, and 138 periodicals were launched, although few survived for long."

Consider some of the names of their papers and note the evangelistic fervor of the publishers: *The Gospel Advocate, The Gospel Banner, The Gospel Fountain, The Universalist Trumpet, The Southern Pioneer, The Southern Evangelist, The Western Evangelist, Light of Zion, Genius of Truth, The Herald of Life, The Herald of Gospel Liberty, The Evangelical Magazine and Gospel Advocate*, and *The Evangelical Universalist*, among others.

Universalist women became active in missionary work shortly after they organized in 1869. One of their goals was to fund extension work both at home and abroad. To that end, the president of the group, Caroline Soule, and another member, Mrs. M. Louise Thomas, sent out thousands of tracts every day all over the world. It was a post office mission, though not called by that name.

Caroline Soule herself, having to travel abroad for her health in 1875, went to England and Scotland. There was already a small group of Universalist churches there that had organized themselves (in 1874) into the Scottish Universalist Convention. While in Scotland she preached a few times and helped dedicate a new church in Stenhousemuir, Larbert. Three years later she returned as a missionary from the women's group, the first foreign Universalist missionary. She started a number of churches and was ordained in 1880 in St. Paul's Universalist Church in Glasgow. It was said that she was "the first woman in all of Europe known to have gained such a status."

She introduced Christmas celebrations for children and encouraged reluctant congregations to sing hymns. She returned to America and other people took her place as missionaries to Scotland. By 1886 she was back in Glasgow, planning to stay only a year, but remaining until her retirement in 1892. She stayed in Scotland until her death in 1903 and kept active in her retirement, holding that "fatigue in the cause of Universalism is infinitely better than inaction, apathy, indolence."

Then there was the Universalist missionary extraordinaire Quillen Hamilton Shinn. Born in 1845 in what became West Virginia, he fought in the Civil War. After the war, he taught school briefly, became converted to Universalism, and graduated from Canton Theological School at St. Lawrence University in 1870. A series of short pastorates in many places followed, in which his love for the missionary enterprise was vividly made manifest.

He gave up the settled ministry in 1890 and for the next five years became an independent missionary for the Universalists,

supporting himself from contributions to his work. Typically
he would arrive in a town, hire a hall to preach in, distribute
leaflets about the meetings, and preach to whoever came, encouraging them to bring new recruits to the next night's meeting. He
always tried to leave some organization in place, whether a church
con-gregation, a Sunday school, a women's group, or a youth group.

In 1895 the denomination employed him as a paid missionary, covering the whole country. After 1900 he concentrated his
efforts in the South. When he died in 1907, he had—Russell
Miller notes—"preached in every state then in the union and at
many points in Canada." He traveled some 25,000 or more miles
each year in this endeavor.

From 1882, he organized national summer meetings, first at
The Weirs in New Hampshire, and later at Ferry Beach in Maine.
These were based on the old midwestern outdoor revival meetings. At first they were mainly preaching events, but they gradually turned into summer educational conferences. In effect,
they were an extension of his missionary efforts, because their
early purpose was to spread the good news of Universalism to all
and sundry.

He was also appointed as national organizer of the Young
People's Christian Union, and one of the projects he encouraged
them to undertake was a Post Office Mission, similar to the work
being done by the Unitarians. When he died, memorial services
were held throughout the country in tribute to this one-man
"missionary army." The denomination built a memorial church
in his honor in Chattanooga, Tennessee.

It is hard to measure the effectiveness of Shinn's work. His
technique of leaving something in place in each community
became known as "the Missouri Plan," because he first began it
there. He did acquaint thousands of persons with the ideas of
Universalism; he recruited hundreds of people to work in his
various groups; he was responsible for building about forty
churches; and he encouraged thirty people to become Universalist ministers. How many of us do as much?

Young people got into the mission act too. Shinn and another minister, Charles Ellwood Nash, had encouraged the National Young People's Christian Union (YPCU) to become active in extension work, especially in building new churches. From 1890 until 1916, they raised money to help in the construction of a number of churches. It was suggested that each member give a dollar a year for mission efforts. Nash pointed out that that was only two cents a week. This "two-cents-a-week for missions" scheme was a great success. Over 170,000 envelopes had been distributed by 1895, and considerable revenue was collected each year. Eventually, a permanent fund was established from this income, which by 1929 was called the Permanent Church Extension Fund.

The young people even came up with $13,000 to sponsor an itinerant Universalist preacher in Texas where he was "to engage in Biblical proof-text debates" with the orthodox. When Shinn founded a black church in the little community of Bartow, Georgia, the YPCU supported it as well as its black preacher, John Murphy, who had been converted to Universalism by our tracts.

The urge to spread Universalism overseas to distant lands excited various people from 1882 on. Thomas B. Thayer agitated in favor of missions overseas. Finally a committee was appointed in 1886 to look into the possibilities, and the next year they reported that Japan looked the most promising. They began to raise money, and by 1890 a vessel bearing three Universalist missionaries docked in Yokohama, Japan.

Dr. George Perin was the leader, 35 years old, vigorous, and able. He proved an ideal choice. Although Perin had to retire in 1894, he left the mission well established. Parishes were organized, native preachers and assistants were added to the staff, and Sunday schools were started. A monthly paper was printed in Japanese, and in 1902 the Blackmer Home was erected as a school for girls. Lucien Blackmer was a Vermont Universalist who was a very generous supporter of the mission work.

The Japanese mission was given great publicity within the denomination. A 1902 cover of *The Universalist Leader* showed ten people on the mission staff, three of whom were women and five of whom were Japanese converts. The Universalist women in America had been supporting the Japanese project liberally, but gradually their interests and money concentrated on the work done at the Blackmer Girls' Home. Catherine Osborn, later joined by M. Agnes Hathaway, was sponsored by the women's group, and the two became faithful pillars of the work at Blackmer Home. Georgene Bowen later joined the staff at Blackmer. By 1913, the women were entirely supporting the work at Blackmer, releasing General Convention money for other aspects of the mission project.

After twenty-five years of work in Japan, the retiring director, Gideon Keirns, felt that the mission had passed through four phases: a rapid expansion during the first five years, a period of testing in the second five years, then a ten-year period of contraction when many of the preaching stations had to be closed, and finally a period of renewal. After twenty-five years of work, the mission could report four places where services were held every Sunday and two occasional preaching stations. There were five native ministers and four American missionaries. The educational work was strong, with 350 youngsters in the Sunday school and about 500 church members in total.

Samuel Ayers was the next mission leader. He labored hard to rebuild the fine brick Central Church in Tokyo. Hardly had the repairs been completed when the Great Earthquake of 1923 struck Tokyo and totally demolished the church. Henry Cary was the next person chosen to replace Ayers, arriving with his family in 1924 and working tirelessly until his death in 1936.

A policy of the mission from the first had been to involve local people as much as possible. In 1925 they formed a Japan Council to direct the project, and by 1932 this was reorganized as the Japanese Universalist Convention.

The passage of the Japanese Religious Organization bill in 1940 forced all groups with less than fifty churches to disband or merge. Consequently, the Universalists put their churches into the care of the Congregational fellowship, while the programs in the schools and social centers continued under the local Japanese leadership.

World War II destroyed Blackmer Home and Dojin House, where the Ohayo kindergarten had been located. The kindergarten relocated to a Quonset hut and continued with a busy program. The Reverend Carleton Fisher visited Japan in 1950 to assess the situation. He recommended a new intercultural approach in which the universal insights of both East and West would be shared. The Reverend John Shidara, who had been ordained in 1934, carried on in a small church at Komegane, a remote village in the Central Japan Alps region. The Universalist Church of America supported the work there and in 1952 helped to rebuild the Universalist Center in Tokyo. In 1990, the Dojin Christian Church in Tokyo, once again an independent Universalist church, observed its centennial. So, in much reduced circumstances, the work continues.

In the heyday of the Universalist mission, there was a vain attempt to start a similar enterprise in Korea. After a feeble start, this came to nothing. The Universalists even tried to start a mission in Cuba at Columbia-on-the-Bay, under the leadership of the Reverend Jacob Straub. This was a cooperative endeavor with Methodists, Baptists, and Presbyterians. Straub assured Boston that "Universalism is in Cuba to stay and to grow," but this proved not to be the case. Perhaps the whole endeavor was too much of a mulligan stew.

The years of the second world war once again put a cramp on all extension efforts overseas or at home. But the end of the war brought fresh efforts to develop new Universalist churches. The Massachusetts Universalist Convention took a major role in this extension work under the leadership of Dr. Clinton Lee Scott. Several new congregations were started. The Universalist movement had dwindled greatly, but under Robert Cummins's leadership they copied many of the programs of the stronger Unitarians in such areas as an organization to meet the needs of isolated religious liberals, a Universalist Service Committee, and a small extension program.

Bring Them Hope, Not Hell

They continued, too, an interest in overseas congregations. In 1952, an ordained minister in the Philippines, the Reverend Toribio S. Quimada, who had been introduced to Universalism, reached out to them and eventually affiliated his congregations with the Unitarian Church of America. Today twenty-six congregations and twenty-four ministers, all on the islands of Negros, Panay, and Mindanao, are associated with the UUA.

In the Universalist success was hidden their decline. Once most mainstream denominations accepted the concept that God was love and that hell was an unnecessary, useless, and harmful invention, the energy behind the spread of Universalism began to fade.

Unitarians came only gradually to sense the need for evangelism in spreading their doctrine. They had begun as a liberalizing idea within a mainstream denomination in New England. Their belief was that God was a unity and not broken up into three confusing pieces. There was much more immediate power in the liberating concept of Universalism than in the liberalizing idea of Unitarianism.

As a result, by the 1830s and 1840s Universalism was more widespread and accepted than was Unitarianism. On the other hand, Unitarians embraced the idea of evangelism somewhat hesitatingly and never wholeheartedly. When the evangelistic spirit moved them, they were more genteel than their Universalist brothers and sisters.

One of the principal reasons for organizing the American Unitarian Association (AUA) in 1825 was to spread the Unitarian idea through the press. Unitarian faith was promulgated largely in the printed word—Universalist faith was expressed in the spoken word.

Support for missionary efforts was split among the Unitarians. The older ministers and lay people, particularly Bostonians, had limited denominational feeling and did not believe in such evangelizing. The Boston churches gave almost no support to denominational causes. One leading merchant was afraid that if they publicized the good news about Unitarianism, the religion might become popular. Even Channing, the year before he died, declared that he was little of a Unitarian. But the younger men were eager and zealous for spreading the "good news" of a Christianity free from the errors of Calvinism. They wanted effective missionary action, and they prevailed.

The way to do it, they felt, was to publish tracts or pamphlets, so one of the stated purposes of the American Unitarian Association was "to diffuse the knowledge and promote the interests of pure Christianity." In its first year the Association published six pamphlets and distributed 17,000 copies of them. By the third year they had twenty-one tracts in print and had sold 143,000 of them. Note that: selling them, not giving them away. They were, after all, Yankees.

In 1826, concerned by the many poor people pouring into the city of Boston, the Association employed the Reverend Joseph Tuckerman to be a minister-at-large to serve these new immigrants. His work was funded largely by women. This program continued until 1834 when the Benevolent Fraternity of Unitarian Churches was organized and took it over.

That same summer a group of students from the Harvard Divinity School volunteered to spend part of their vacation exploring possible areas where new churches could be started in Massachusetts. The Association also sent a man they called a "messenger" to see if there was any interest in the developing western territories for new Unitarian churches. Mr. Moses G. Thomas, a student at the Divinity School, went as a special agent covering well over 4,000 miles, part of the way on horseback, and reported back that there were good prospects in many midwestern towns for the establishment of a new Unitarian church. The immediate lack was of ministers to serve them.

The next year the Unitarian Book and Tract Society was organized to supply tracts free, rather than charging for them. The Unitarian Sunday School Society was organized the same year to help with the education of the oncoming generation.

From 1815 on, Unitarianism seemed to be advancing rapidly everywhere. This disturbed that orthodox clergyman, the Reverend Lyman Beecher, and he took a church in the North End of Boston and conducted crowded revival meetings to strengthen the old Calvinistic religion. It was helpful for the Unitarians to have such sharp competition lest they become too complacent.

By 1837 the AUA had decided it needed a full-time secretary, and the Reverend Charles Briggs took the position and held it until 1849. He placed the missionary effort on a regular footing. In 1840 men were sent as scouts into nine states to see if they could get new churches started. Much interest was shown, but still Boston was unable to provide the needed ministers. Nevertheless, congregations were gathered in Cincinnati, Louisville, St. Louis, Detroit, and Chicago. In 1825 there had been 125 churches that could be called Unitarian. By 1850 that number had increased to 230.

Interest in foreign missions was kindled in 1854 by the Reverend Charles Brooks. Charles H. A. Dall sailed for India in 1855. His instructions read, "You go out as a Unitarian missionary because we have reason to believe that many will receive the gospel as we hold it. . . . But you are not expected to carry mere doctrinal discussions and sectarian strifes to those distant lands." He worked there for thirty years, starting several churches and schools. No successor could be found for him after his death in 1886. At the same time a mission was started among the Chippewa Indians in Minnesota and carried on for two years.

The Western Unitarian Conference was organized in 1852 in Cincinnati to encourage church extension in that expanding midsection of the country. There were less than a dozen Unitarian churches widely scattered throughout that region and separated also by the extreme difficulties of travel. William Greenleaf Eliot, the Conference's first president, stressed that missionary activity should be one of its primary goals. In spite of the upheaval caused by the Civil War, the churches in the area tripled to thirty-five by its end.

During the Civil War years, interest in missionary efforts was at a low ebb, particularly in the East, as all attention was concentrated on the war. Sixty Unitarian ministers served as chaplains or soldiers or worked in the Sanitary Commission that Dr. Bellows had created.

After the war, the AUA kept a missionary secretary in the West to start churches, but the Western Conference had its own separate missionary funds and missionaries. Jenkin Lloyd Jones was one of these. He was appointed a part-time missionary secretary in 1875, and five years later—so effective had his work been—he was made full time. During his career, Jones traveled more than 100,000 miles spreading Unitarianism. When he finished his work, there were twice as many churches as when he started. There were also seven new state conferences.

After the war there was a great renewal of energy in the denomination. The National Conference of Unitarian Churches was organized. It assisted the AUA in establishing churches in college towns where they felt there was a chance to influence the oncoming generation. At this time churches in centers like Ann Arbor, Michigan, and Ithaca, New York, were organized. Unitarian churches revived in the South. The number of churches in the Western Conference doubled within a year. A score of missionary preachers were sent out, holding meetings in over a hundred towns and cities, and from this missionary effort eight new churches resulted.

Even Boston had a home mission program designed to reach people not already attending existing churches. The Reverend George Hepworth, a preacher with great popular gifts, was employed, and he held a series of crowded religious meetings in the largest theater in the city. Similar meetings were held in other large cities until the novelty wore off.

Meanwhile, the denomination endeavored to strengthen what were seen as weak points. In 1876 money was contributed to build a suitable church in Washington, DC. A memorial church in honor of Channing was erected at Newport, Rhode Island. The mortgage on the struggling New Orleans church was assumed by the AUA, and in 1886 a handsome headquarters building for the denomination was built in Boston.

At the same time, educational work in the South was carried

on; aid was sent to both Hungary and India; and the Reverend Henry Bond, who earlier had worked with the Ute Indians, was sent to establish an Industrial School for the Crow Indians in Montana.

The Post Office Mission was an example of quiet Unitarian evangelism. The work commenced as early as 1877. The founder of the project was Sallie Ellis. She sent out pamphlets and tracts about Unitarianism to inquirers all over the country, and she did this volunteer work even though she was elderly, poor, and an invalid. Besides sending out tracts she wrote what came to be known as "Cheerful Letters." Gradually the task became too much for one person, and she enlisted the help of other women. Eventually, the work was taken over by the office of the Western Unitarian Conference in Chicago, and volunteers came in daily to answer the many requests. The Conference published both Unity Short Tracts and Unity Mission Tracts to use in this work.

When the General Alliance of Unitarian Women was formed in 1880, one of their main goals was to stimulate and improve "the charitable and missionary work" of Unitarianism. Their first cooperative project was to assist in this Post Office Mission. Sending out religious literature had been done before: Edward Everett Hale's church in Boston had sent material to correspondents all over the country, and, even earlier, pamphlets had been distributed by the Dorchester Female Tract Society. But now, under the auspices of the General Alliance it became a national project.

In time many city churches organized their own Post Office Mission committees. The women of King's Chapel in Boston took on the Cheerful Letter project too, editing a monthly paper with that name, and sending it to shut-ins, along with books, sewing and writing materials, seeds and bulbs, greeting cards, and simple holiday parcels. This work continued for some time under the leadership of Lilian Freeman Clarke, Dr. James Freeman Clarke's daughter. The Cheerful Letters committee became a project of the General Alliance and also included setting up libraries in communities where there were none. By 1924, some 150 such libraries had been started, mostly within the United States, but some in the Philippines, the Virgin Islands, and Japan. Years later, when the Alliance was no longer carrying on the Post Office Mission, the project was continued in somewhat altered form by the Church of the Larger Fellowship.

An invitation came from Japanese citizens to send a representative who would explain Unitarianism to them, and in 1888, the Reverend Arthur Knapp was sent. His mandate was "to meet with, to encourage, and to cooperate with any individual or groups of persons in Japan who might wish to know the more advanced thought of Christendom about the spiritual problems and interests of man."

A year later he returned to Boston full of enthusiasm and enlisted six preachers and teachers to go back with him to continue the mission, "not to convert, but to confer." Large audiences were drawn to lectures and sermons, a magazine was started, tracts published, and a training school was started. A Japanese Unitarian Association was organized and in 1894 a headquarters, Unity Hall, was built in Tokyo. Knapp returned home and turned over the leadership of the mission to the Reverend Clay MacCauley. MacCauley served as field worker for a total of twenty-one years (1889–1900 and 1909–1919) and became a kind of elder statesman to the mission. The AUA closed the mission in 1921.

In 1918 Henry Hallam Saunderson introduced the idea of the Wayside Pulpit to the United States. It was based on the model developed in England and Canada. It consisted of a sharp, pithy sentence, printed on a poster, and displayed outside a subscribing church on its bulletin board during the week. It was a means of preaching to people who otherwise never would have ventured inside the church. And in many instances, it did bring people into the church. It was one more quiet tool of extension.

After the First World War, emphasis on Unitarian growth was renewed. This was led by the Laymen's League, rather than the AUA or the National Conference, and they turned to an ex-Roman Catholic for help.

William Lawrence Sullivan, the minister of All Souls Unitarian Church in New York City, came from an unusual background. He had grown up as a Roman Catholic and was ordained to the priesthood in 1899, when he was twenty-seven years old. For two years he was a mission-preacher for the Paulists, then served as professor of theology at St. Thomas College. He became deeply involved in the Modernist movement, but when this was condemned by Pope Pius X, he became disillusioned with the Roman Catholic church and in 1909 left the priesthood. He had already been attracted to the ideas of the English Unitarian, James Martineau, and soon joined the Unitarian Church in Cleveland, Ohio. In 1912 he was fellowshipped as a Unitarian minister. A powerful and effective preacher, by 1916 Samuel Eliot had arranged for Sullivan to conduct a missionary tour of the West coast.

This was highly successful and during the next few years Sullivan often went off for a week's preaching mission to some community. In 1922 he was asked to become the full-time Missionary Minister of the Unitarian Laymen's League. He resigned from All Souls and spent the next three years touring the country as a missionary at large. Many places requested his services, and he conducted missions all over the United States and Canada. He concluded this phase of his service in 1924.

When Louis Craig Cornish took over in 1927 as AUA president, one of his goals was to establish five new churches each year. He brought in Charles R. Joy to assist in this project. Studies were made of appropriate sites, and a number of churches were organized, which exist to this day. But the Great Depression intervened making it impossible to fund such work, and in 1931 the board of directors voted to suspend the effort.

The Church of the Larger Fellowship was founded in 1944 and provides a ministry to isolated religious liberals throughout the world, offering them a spiritual home within the Unitarian Universalist movement. With 2,200 members, today it is the largest church in the denomination. It takes an active role in extension efforts.

Frederick May Eliot saw the need for expanding Unitarianism. Remembering the old concept of Unitarian Lay Centers, he proposed—after World War II—the establishment of groups of religious liberals led by lay people. Under the direction of Lon Ray Call and Munroe Husbands, the Unitarian Fellowship movement was launched in 1948. In ten years, one-third of the denomination's increase came from the many fellowships that Husbands established in his wide-ranging travels. Many of these have since become churches.

◆ ◆ ◆ ◆

In this brief account of Universalist and Unitarian extension efforts, I have not included the work done since the merger of the two denominations in 1961. Suffice it to say extension work has continued with varying emphasis in the past thirty-odd years. The fellowship effort continued; the Church of the Larger Fellowship has developed a "Church-on-Loan" program; during Dana Greeley's presidency, the Ministers-on-Loan program was introduced; Christopher Raible initiated the Sharing in Growth program; Ronald Clark conceived the plan of the Extension ministry; Joan Goodwin, with the assistance of Thomas Chulak and William Hamilton-Holway, developed the New Congregation program; and Charles Gaines has given special attention to midsized and large-sized congregations, along with all the regular, continuous work of the Extension Department.

Many people have been unaware of the evangelical work that has been done, and continues to be done, in our denomination. Even though we have seldom talked about it, this missionary work has been essential to our good health and continued growth.

Evangelistes is a Greek word that means "the bringer of good news." But Unitarian Universalists are "bearers of the best news." For we are the optimists in religion, we believe in the enormous possibilities in human nature. We do not, as John Murray said so long ago, wish to push people deeper into theological despair. We are not like the pessimistic Calvinists who can only see sin and evil wherever they look and who worship a God they believe damns most of His own creatures.

Although Unitarian Universalists see clearly the crimes and faults of human beings, we also see, as Channing said, their " kind affections," their "struggles against oppression," their "achievements in science and art," their "examples of heroic and saintly virtues." We are not the nay-sayers of life. We are the bearers of a larger hope. We are on the side of the universe. We bring hope and courage, not hell and despair, to the religious arena.

*Modern
Perspectives
on Evangelism*

Out of the Sidelines and Into the Main Streets

Steps Toward
an Evangelical
Unitarian Universalism

Lawrence X. Peers

THE WORD "EVANGELISM" is not even permitted in the religious vocabulary of most contemporary Unitarian Universalists. Not only do we have a severe allergy to the word, we also resist any activity that would give the appearance of "proselytizing" or promoting our religious faith with fervor. Obviously, there are some well-founded reasons for eschewing some of the attitudes and behaviors that we tend to associate with evangelism, especially the excesses and abuses of some prominent televangelists. Yet to dissociate ourselves from evangelism in such a blanket way not only limits our options as a religious movement, but may also limit the further development of our Unitarian Universalist faith.

Time and again, when I do premarital counseling with a couple or when I meet with a group of prospective members in a congregation, I encounter the refrain, "if only I had known about Unitarian Universalism sooner." I recognize that for a variety of reasons, as Unitarian Universalists we tend to wait until people wash upon our shores before we tell them about our religious faith and our religious community. We have been well intentioned all these years. We may have also been misguided. I feel that the time has come for us to appropriate an understanding of evangelism that can help move Unitarian Universalism out of the sidelines of the religious world and into the main streets. Yet, we would be naive to think that we can appropriate evangelism into our religious style as Unitarian Universalism without some honest re-examination of our assumptions and attitudes and some deliberate changes in our self-limiting behaviors. Such a process requires at least some of the steps that I have outlined here.

1. *Acknowledge our own negative associations to evangelism.* Whenever I begin a discussion with a group of Unitarian Universalists on the topic of evangelism, I usually begin by asking the group to free associate with the word "evangelism." It takes no time at all for the words to be flung through the air as I desperately try to write them down. One recognizes right away that our rational Unitarian Universalist persona dissipates when we touch a nerve that can hold pain in some lives and promote arrogance in others.

One group of Unitarian Universalists that I asked recently to participate in this exercise elicited a long list of words including: "loud suits," "big hair," "big teeth," "big business," "greed and systematic manipulation," "invasion," "right wing," "denial of sex," "hypocrisy," and "narrow minds." In the midst of all the genuine humor that the exercise often evokes, there is usually also a great deal of pain and anger. In the midst of all the emotion conveyed by the words and the tones by which they are communicated, there was also a sense of arrogance and distancing from a style of religion that seems an anathema to most of us as Unitarian Universalists. Indeed, even beyond the specific content of the words that make up the list is the force by which the reactions to the word flow forth from the group. This force must be reckoned with and eventually rechanneled into some appropriate attitudes and behaviors that will free us as Unitarian Universalists to give fuller expression to our own our fervor and compassion for religious seekers. A necessary first step, I feel, is to allow people to own some of their negative connotations with the word "evangelism." This recognition prepares the way for moving toward some appropriation of an evangelism that can be congruent with our cherished Unitarian Universalist values and approach to the religious search.

2. *Owning our own guiding values.*
In order to dramatize how distanced most of us feel from the negative connotations with the word "evangelism," at the end of the word-association exercise, I usually take the sheet on which I've written their words, roll it up into a ball, and throw it into the group. This is the place, I suspect, that many of us would have ended the discussion and feel satisfied. I believe, however, that it is just the beginning of the discussion.

Though our judgments about evangelism are explicit, underlying these negative reactions must be some strong positive opinions about how religion *should* be shared. These tacit opinions are often implied in our negative reactions to evangelism. When given the opportunity, most people are able to express these opinions directly.

After the word-association exercise, I usually challenge the group to develop guidelines for sharing our faith that *are* congruent with our particular approach to religion. We have often as Unitarian Universalists divorced ourselves from any considerations like this. Yet, slowly but surely, the group is able to name some of the guidelines for a Unitarian Universalist evangelism. Here are a few typical responses:

1. Talk with pride and enthusiasm.
2. Look for opportunities for dialogue.
3. Welcome questions about the Unitarian Universalist faith.
4. State beliefs positively.

5. Be patient and respectful of differing views.
6. Be clear about our core values and demonstrate them in our approach to the conversation about our faith.
7. Live our faith. Let our lives speak.
8. Listen to the other person; ask probing and thoughtful questions.
9. Give a personal testimonial.
10. Because experience is a source of our personal religion-making, listen to the other person's experience and also share your own.

This list also reveals to the participants some of our typical behaviors when Unitarian Universalists are engaged in a conversation with someone about their faith. Oftentimes, what we do is the direct opposite of the behaviors that we have listed here. However, once Unitarian Universalists are prompted to discern ways to share our story with others in ways that are congruent with our approach to our religion, some new possibilities emerge for us. Some of our lame excuses for not "proselytizing" are exposed. It is a humbling experience to realize that our arrogance and our derision of other styles of evangelism do not exempt us from finding a style of evangelism that is expressive of our Unitarian Universalist approach. In fact, how we manifest some of our central values and our approach in these interactions with others can allow for them an experience of Unitarian Universalism that words alone could not convey. We recognize that the responsibility we have to share our faith provides a pathway for others into our religious communities.

3. *Creating pathways to Unitarian Universalist faith and community.*
Once we have discerned some guidelines for sharing our faith that are congruent with Unitarian Universalism, we release ourselves to create activities that will embody these guidelines in our practice as individuals, as congregations, and as an association of congregations.

For many of us, this will mean that we need to create some intentional experiences for learning ways to share our faith with others. In articulating the guiding values for a Unitarian Universalist approach to evangelism, we then are free to experiment with ways to live out those values. Examples include role playing an interaction with a prospective visitor to our church, training in visitation to marginal or prospective members, and opportunities for members to tell their own story and "witness" to their faith.

In addition to these educational events that enable Unitarian Universalists to feel more comfortable and to gain the skills of sharing their faith, there are other practices that help promote outreach and interaction with newcomers and seekers in the community. These might include regular "bring a friend" events in a church, attention to the quality of the newcomer experience, and multiple small groups that relate our Unitarian Universalist faith to specific life issues and concerns.

4. *Creating an evangelizing church.*
Kirk Hadaway, in his book *Church Growth Principles*, delineated the factors that determined whether a church was growing, plateaued, or declining. Among the strongest characteristics of a growing church is a church that has an intentional evangelism program. We may easily quarrel with some of the techniques and styles of evangelism. Nevertheless, we might also be challenged to look at the way an evangelizing church engages in activities that help deepen the faith of its membership, clarifies its mission, provides opportunities for service, and organizes itself for living out its mission in service. Numerical growth is a phenomenon that reflects an ability of a church to want to share and live out its faith in ways that attract others to that essential human enterprise.

Consequently, a myopic view of evangelism is one that views the sole purpose as increasing attention on numbers of members and participants and on the numerical growth of a church. Growth in membership is the most likely result of efforts in evangelism. But numerical growth without accompanying depth and maturation of faith, social outreach, and congregational development cannot sustain itself. Moreover, without these sustaining activities a congregation cannot motivate or mobilize itself toward evangelism, which is a fervent living out and sharing of its faith.

As Loren Mead proposes in his book, *More than Numbers: The Ways Churches Grow*, numerical growth is only one dimension of growth in a church. To sustain numerical growth, a church must also be doing something to help mature the faith of its members. Otherwise, people lose contact with why they are Unitarian Universalists and why they continue to be Unitarian Universalists. Moreover, they are able to communicate more clearly and directly what their faith means to others. To sustain growth means also to attend to and revise the organizational structures of a church in order to encourage involvement and responsiveness in the congregation. A growing congregation is one that seeks to give expression to its faith in some visible ways of care, concern, and creating justice in the world.

Each of these dimensions of growth enhance and reinforce the others. To grow numerically, but to not find ways to mature the faith or involve your members in meaningful arenas of ministry does not sustain growth. To help mature the faith of your members or to be known and visible in the community because of your particular social ministries helps a congregation to continue not only to grow but also to develop as a religious community that is evangelizing by its way of being a church.

Each of these are ways to promote an evangelizing church. For me, a church that is fully expressive of its evangelism is a church that reaches out to others and creates pathways for their involvement in the life and mission of the congregations. An evangelizing church is one that calls forth some of the deepest spiritual yearnings and aspirations among its membership and also knows how to engage that membership in works of transformation and justice in an ailing world. A congregation that is truly evangelizing cannot help but share its good news and allow that good news to impact the lives of others.

The Risk of Evangelism

Evangelism entails a risk for us as Unitarian Universalists. A more deliberate approach to the sharing and living out of our Unitarian Universalist faith calls us to mature our faith in ways that we have not been called upon to do in recent history. It means moving beyond some inhibiting norms.

To make such a journey is to risk discovering how truly universalistic our faith is, after all. It is a risk for us to find ways to communicate our faith in ways that directly touch the hurts and hopes of others. It means not only trying to influence others, but also being open to influence by others. A more deliberate evangelical approach to Unitarian Universalism means that we are willing to test our faith, our values, and our vision in the main streets, where people live and move and have their being.

Evangelism at its heart means the ability to share one's faith in such a way that you offer it as a way of intersecting with the lives of others. Publicity is one strategy in evangelism, but it is not evangelism. Publicity can be a passive, rather than an engaging, activity. Evangelism aims toward much more. It is an encounter between two human beings. Evangelism provides an interaction between a message and a recipient of that message that answers the question: Is this a faith that can truly liberate me? Is this a religious community that can become for me a vehicle of saving grace and healing power? Is this Unitarian Universalism a way toward what is holy? Will this engagement with Unitarian Universalism really make a difference in my life and for this world?

To live up to this definition of evangelism is truly humbling because it moves beyond sharing information and toward engaging in transformative dialogue and service with others. To begin to imagine ourselves as Unitarian Universalists living up to this definition of evangelism means that we challenge ourselves to answer these deeper questions for ourselves as well. Therefore, we must be able to name what has been liberating, healing, transforming about our engagement within Unitarian Universalism. Therefore we must be willing to ask ourselves: How has my involvement within this Unitarian Universalist faith brought me closer to truth, to the holy, or to a healing love? To attempt to engage in evangelism without this kind of introspection is to weaken your message before it even begins to be shared.

Why Bother?

Why even bother? With the risk so high, with our comfort with the status quo so pleasing, why even bother our imaginations enough to consider a Unitarian Universalist evangelism? Simply put, the growth and development of our Unitarian Universalist faith is dependent upon it.

We live in a time that has the largest number of unchurched people than in any previous time. When this unchurched population is interviewed, it is discovered that many of them would be interested in a faith much like that of Unitarian Universalism, if they but knew it. The change in Unitarian Universalism in the last decade or so is that we have become more boldly spiritual in our orientation to worship and programming. There was a time when we distanced ourselves so much from all that seemed "religious" that we prided ourselves in not being "religious." Now that we have more honestly recognized in many of our congregations our spiritual hungers and our spiritual resources, we are subtlely refashioning our Unitarian Universalism. Soon we may be able to eliminate some of the practices that more appropriately fit our self-image as a group of "religious refugees." This, too, will be a bold and creative step.

Such passion and commitment is worthy of Unitarian Universalism. We deserve to move our faith out of the sidelines and into the main streets. It requires more of us than we have often imagined ourselves giving. Yet, it is in living out this passion and commitment that we discover what is ultimately meaningful, healing, and liberating in our lives.

In *Olympia Brown: The Battle for Equality*, Charlotte Coté quotes the Universalist missionary: "We are worthy to be entrusted with this great heritage." I believe that we need to acknowledge more fully what it means for us to be entrusted with this heritage. Furthermore, we need to follow Brown's admonishment to "go on finding new applications of these truths and new enjoyment in their contemplation."

The Bold Witness

Harvey M. Joyner, Jr.

"WE'VE A STORY TO TELL to the Nations" is a gospel hymn that I grew up singing as a Southern Baptist years ago. It is an enthusiastic song about spreading one's faith. Its message is about going forth into our community with the belief that we have a vision for creating a more loveable and liveable world. Though I have outgrown the religiously exclusive language of this song, the emotional vibrancy and the message of "good news" is still present in a faith that, I believe, is powerfully translatable for today's pluralistic society.

Several years ago, I traveled with a group of college classmates on a witnessing campaign to Daytona Beach, Florida. It was spring break and the Home Mission Board of the Southern Baptist Convention thought it would be a great thing for us zealous undergraduates to promote "the faith" among the sun bunnies and the water worshipers there on the sands of the Florida Atlantic coast. Once there, we were primed with training seminars each morning, guiding us in how to proselytize strangers who were at the beach for reasons other than religion. It was a tough week for me! Somehow, even then, I felt that it was wrong to try to "convert" or "change" others to a particular religious persuasion. So, while some took this missionary endeavor seriously, while many others had fun in the sun, I wrestled intensely with my conscience. As it turned out, I spent most of my week helping with the Red Cross shelter that had been set up there as a beach-front coffee house.

Somewhere during what seemed to be an awfully long week, I stumbled into a pamphlet-toting preacher on the boardwalk. In our brief visit, I asked this young man to tell me something about his life story, to which he replied, "Read the tract! It's in the tract!" One quick glance at his printed material told me that his story was missing, unless he was Jesus Christ himself! Before I could pursue further conversation with this beach-front missionary, he was off peddling his neatly packaged religion elsewhere.

So often we religious liberals have reacted with such revulsion to the stereotypic boardwalk preacher that we have neglected our own need to do mission outreach. If our "evangel" is a gospel of healthily integrating choice with justice, then why are we not "out there" telling any and everyone in our community about it? Instead of ridiculing fundamentalists for their seemingly boundless zeal and their overly simplistic answers, why are we smugly content with our self-description as "the best kept secret in town?" Our story is rich with the personalities of those who have suffered, bled, and died that we might inherit a legacy of freedom and promise. Our cause is for the enhancement of human dignity and for creating inclusive circles of love. That is our gospel. That is our good news. Isn't it about time that we go tell it on the mountain?

First of all, we need to see evangelism as a positive activity, as an aggressive activity. Instead of waiting for the people to come hear us in our church house, we must see evangelism as something we "do as we go." It is the kind of evangelism that takes place in the normal flow of our everyday life. The *sine qua non* for "telling the good news" is the personal faith of the evangelist. If one does not have one's own faith house in order, one is not at all likely to want to be an evangelist. You cannot share your faith if you do not have a faith to share. This applies to pastors as well as to everyone else.

It is not necessary to have all the answers in order to be effective in evangelism. It is crucial, however, to know what one believes, to be emotionally honest, and to know how to articulate one's beliefs to others. Faith is a gift, not an academic achievement. Yet all of us are called to be stewards of life's gifts. We are also obligated to share our faith.

Part of our reluctance, as Unitarian Universalists, for sharing our faith publicly is that we are unclear about our own particular spiritual identity. Bold witnessing, effective evangelism, calls for spiritual clarity! Once and for all, let us dispel the notion that, as Unitarian Universalists, we have created a new, utopic religion. Rather, we are a religious institution, an association of diverse congregations and fellowships, whose primary focus is responding ethically to the culture in which we find ourselves. Each of us, even if we have difficulty articulating it, are Unitarian Universalist Christians, Unitarian Universalist Jews, Unitarian Universalist Humanists, Unitarian Universalist Pagans, or Unitarian Universalist whatever else. The fuzzy-headedness of blenderizing "a little bit of this, that, and the other" makes for poor evangelism. If we are serious about celebrating diversity, we must come to see that progress happens only when we honor differences.

Much of the recent growth with All Souls Unitarian Church in Colorado Springs has happened because of conscious efforts to embody diversity, rather than to homogenize everyone into the lowest common denominator so as to create a liberal orthodoxy of sameness. As a multifaith congregation, we are finding diversity a stimulus toward further growth. With a Humanist Association, a Covenant of UU Pagans, a Christian Fellowship, and, hopefully, other spiritual subgroups to follow, we are coming to see ourselves as a microcosmic interfaith body, a congregation of many religious points of view, yet covenanted with one another in a spirit of trust, hope, and love. This diversity finds expression both in style and substance within worship events, religious education, and within the spiritual intimacy groups that regularly meet. The "good news" of Unitarian Universalism is that it gives us a "safe house" in which to wage our own heresy, whatever tradition we might have come from. Any meaningful dialogue we have requires that we acknowledge and respect others to be as they are, because how they are serves them and their particular life experience.

Being a member of a multifaith church in no way requires us to surrender the uniqueness of our particular faith. It does not require us to be less Christian, less Jewish, less humanist, less pagan, less whatever else. What it does demand is an openness to the truth regardless of its source, an awareness that others possess insights that might have escaped us.

The challenge among Unitarian Universalists today is that we move beyond a perfunctory liberalism to a universalist faith that is generously liberal. In order to be bold witnesses within the larger community, we must move beyond a generic faith to a religious literacy and spiritual grounding in our own chosen faith. My testimony is that, as we do this, the barriers of suspicion and distrust are exchanged for a faith that values and respects those who are different. Somehow, in welcoming the "otherness," religious, political, cultural, and otherwise, we are able to become more connected to that source which nurtures and empowers us for the work of ministry.

In addition to spiritual clarity, bold witnessing calls for emotional honesty. Unitarian Universalists have to be some of the most emotionally pent-up people that I know. Speaking as one who has had to deal, not only with a gender-based conditioning of emotional repression, but also with the emotionally loaded issues of my life, I ran into a highly rationalized approach to faith. In my religious odyssey from Southern Baptist to Presbyterian and then to Unitarian Universalist, the priority of "what I think" took precedence over "what I feel."

The potential difficulty that arises from an academically and intellectually grounded spirituality is that we tend to limit the emotional expression of our faith. Threatened by intimacy, many of us consistently maneuver to keep a certain distance from people, preferring instead objectivity and rational analysis. Our weakness tends to be in the expression of what we feel. Yet healing and wholeness call for the healthy interpretation and expression of intellect and emotions. Yes, it does matter that our faith has intellectual integrity. And, yes, it also matters that we have a faith that is emotionally expressive.

Whether "amening" in the worship service, or simply affirming the contributions of someone in a business meeting, emotional honesty is a way to reprogram ourselves individually, and as a church, for more positive results in our lives. As William Blake once put it, "The tygers of wrath are wiser than the horses of instruction." In addition to anger, I suspect that emotional wisdom has to do with a full range of feelings. Verbalization of feelings encourages others to open up and share their joys, sorrows, and vulnerabilities, too. Of all the places in the world that I know, the church needs to be a "safe place" for emotional tears, for diffusing anger, for conquering "n"th-degree fears, and for celebrating our joys. I am convinced that our message of faith, hope, and love needs to be something that we are excited about. Enough of this dry lecture stuff. Our gospel needs to be emotionally vibrant so that we enthusiastically look for ways to tell others about how our faith has made a difference in our lives!

In the late eighteenth and early nineteenth centuries, the Unitarian-Trinitarian split within congregationalism had its roots in the period of the so-called Great Awakening. A firm opposition to revivalism and the whole pietistic emphasis on a religion of the heart was a settled conviction among liberals. Revivalism, with its emphasis on first-time conversion, tended to be more interested in the experiential evidence than in the intellectual quality of faith. The extremes of revivalism displayed themselves in extended outdoor camp meetings, around-the-clock preaching, praying, and hymn-singing, frequently accompanied by ecstatic manifestations, such as trances, jerking, barking like dogs, and profuse weeping. The extremes of rationalism displayed themselves in terms of ethical maxims with a focus on social action. Promoting a social gospel, minus God-language, the tendency was toward achieving our potential through the use of reason and the scientific method.

My response to the revivalist-rationalist controversy is that this is not a problem to be solved, but a polarity to be managed wisely. Today, as we swiftly move into the twenty-first century, the challenge is to balance personal transformation with social action, to embrace both emotional openness and intellectual integrity in our faith development. But, because of our rationalistic history, we Unitarian Universalists seem to be struggling to reclaim emotional honesty so that we might be better at saying what we feel. The time has come and is long overdue for us to demonstrate evangelical fervor about our "good news" to a world desperate for heralds of personal choice and social responsibility.

Not only does bold witnessing require spiritual clarity and emotional honesty, it also calls for mission outreach. As theologian Emil Brunner put it, "The church exists by mission as fire exists by burning." The mission of the church has always been defined as everything we are sent into the world to do. This includes evangelism and service, word and action. Mission outreach involves carrying the gifts of love and respect to people wherever they are, working for a better world with social and political structures that reflect the inherent worth and dignity of all people. So it is crucial that we understand church and mission as inseparable. There is no church without mission nor mission without the church. And the agent of our mission outreach, though called by many names and left nameless by some, is the very soul of our existence, working through us to redeem a broken world.

Mission outreach calls for announcing our presence and our message within the community in which we live. Only a few years ago, here in Colorado Springs, we seized the opportunity to become involved with the Unitarian Universalist Association's media campaign entitled "A Religion That Puts Its Faith in You!" This effort included a local Growth and Development Team, print advertisements from our Public Relations Office in Boston that were printed in the various newspapers in town, and targeted radio announcement spots. Along with the media blitz, we shored up details for Sunday's event by volunteer-staffing a visitor's table, recruiting Sunday greeters, going to two worship services with concomitant religious education programs, and even placing a large, colorful "Welcome" banner above the front entryway of our church. All of these little things have contributed in a big way toward being a bold, yet inviting witness in downtown Colorado Springs. Our membership has more than doubled in the past five years, and we just recently launched a second congregation in the northeast sector of our city. Announcing ourselves and our message has created a revival of Unitarian Universalism in Colorado Springs, something this town had not witnessed for over a century.

Mission outreach also calls for a commitment to social justice in the here and now. Colorado Springs, a city of 300,000, with over sixty para-church ministries, has become a capital city for right-wing Christianity over the last decade. Although this has seemed an obnoxious thorn in the flesh to many, the conservative family-values crowd has rendered us a golden opportunity. We have been picketed, bomb-threatened, and harassed for public statements against censorship; for supporting women's reproductive rights; for providing advocacy for the lesbian, gay, and bisexual community; and for protests against the Persian Gulf War. The noise brought on by these issues in our community has been a wake-up call to those who had been religiously asleep and who now are coming to us seeking support and empowerment.

This ministry in Colorado Springs has given our church an opportunity to denounce institutions and practices that wound and oppress people. We have had significant members of our congregation write letters to the editor, serve on public debate panels, and march in civic parades promoting racial, sexual, and religious justice. In this struggle to address the dangers that threaten our world, we have discovered an ancient truth—whoever gives his or her life for the sake of love and justice will find it! Somehow, in the struggle to do the right thing, we have found a church that is both religious and liberal, universal and empowering.

In addition to announcing ourselves and taking a stand for social justice, mission outreach calls us to tell others about the "good news" of our faith. Our multifaith church affords us the room for freedom of belief, respect of those different from ourselves, and opportunities to enact our responsibility toward others and our world.

Our "great commission" as liberal evangelists is to witness "as we go, wherever we go." The opportunities to tell others about our church and about our rich, diverse story of faith need to be seized within the natural course of events. This kind of lifestyle evangelism is done "as we go" and "as the spirit leads." Visiting with a neighbor, talking with those in our work-a-day lives, participating in various volunteer activities, even our family times, afford us numerous opportunities to speak a good word about the Unitarian Universalist approach to life and faith. As late-eighteenth-century Universalist preacher John Murray put it,

> Go out into the highways and byways. Give the people something of your new vision. You possess only a small light, but uncover it, let it shine, use it in order to bring more light and understanding to the hearts and minds of men and women. Give them, not hell, but hope and courage; preach the kindness and everlasting love of God.

As we go about telling others of our unique ministry and message, let us remember that it is not our job to convert anybody. Our job is simply to be who we are. Our job is to shine our light as a beacon for those who are looking to share our path on the return trip home to healing and wholeness. Despite all the differences between us, we are called in our various ways to say and do basically the same thing, because we are motivated to bear witness, in word and action, to the same spirit of love that nurtures and empowers us.

Harvey M. Joyner, Jr.

When it comes to being a bold witness of our faith, it is not simply "Read the tract! It's in the tract!" Rather, the story we have to tell is in, and of, our lives. That story, precious and unique as it is, deserves to be told!

Courting the Baby Boomers

Suzanne P. Meyer

SHE IS A FORTY-YEAR-OLD, divorced professional. Today, she sits curled up on the sofa in the minister's office of her UU church and recounts her spiritual journey. It is a familiar story, one that parallels the journeys of 76 million of her peers born between 1947 and 1961. She is a member of the birth cohort known collectively as the post-World War II baby boom. And her story is of vital interest to those Unitarian Universalist congregations that are seriously committed to evangelism.

She was born in late 1953, smack in the middle of the baby boom, or right on the cusp that separates the members of the first wave of the boom from those born after 1954, who make up the second wave of the boom. (I'll refer to those two groups later as first-wave boomers and second-wave boomers.) Like so many of her peers, she attended over-crowded public schools and graduated from a high school class that included over 700 seniors. After graduation, she moved away from home to attend a large, impersonal state university.

The Vietnam War, the assassinations of the Kennedys and Martin Luther King, Jr., Watergate, and the women's movement were the key events that shaped her worldview just as the Great

Baby Boomers

Depression, World War II, and the cold war were the events that shaped the worldview of her parents.

In terms of formal church affiliation, she attended Sunday school regularly as a child and took part in the youth choir. She remarks: "I would say church played a big role in my life as a child, but when I got to be a teenager, I lost interest. In the late sixties church wasn't exactly 'hip,' if you know what I mean. I did not even think about going back to church until I was in my late twenties and then I did not even seriously consider going back to a church of my parent's denomination."

She was invited to a Unitarian Universalist church by a friend and was drawn back again and again because of the church's liberal stance on social justice issues. "I was involved in anti-death penalty work at the time. I had just moved to a relatively small, conservative southern town, I didn't know many people, and it was hard to connect with others who shared my values. The Unitarian Universalist church was just about the only place I felt free to discuss my interests. The social concerns committee in the church became my support group. Later on as a divorced person living a long way from home, church became my extended family. You know, for celebrating the holidays and things like that."

Her spiritual journey is a familiar journey not only because *she* is *me,* but also because my experience has much in common with that of the other baby boom members of my congregation. As a Unitarian Universalist parish minister and a baby boomer, I am keenly interested in what my church can do to attract and minister to the 76 million Americans who were born between 1947 and 1961.

I began this chapter with my own story because I am convinced the best way for us, as clergy and laypersons, to understand the baby boomers and to recognize their unique set of needs is to listen to their stories with careful attention paid to the descriptions of the key institutions and events that shaped their lives.

The needs and expectations of many of the boomers are

significantly different from the needs and expectations of previous generations of Unitarian Universalists. And yet, *Newsweek* magazine described Unitarian Universalism as the quintessential baby boomer church. This raises the question, Is there a relationship between baby boomers and Unitarian Universalism? And, if so, What can this mean to us in terms of church growth?

A discussion of church growth and baby boomers must begin with a profile of the typical person born between 1947 and 1961. A word of caution: be advised that any discussion of baby boomers, Unitarian Universalism, and church growth must include not only a profile of the boomer generation, but also the caveat that the influx of boomers in your church may bring about changes that the church members born before 1947 may find difficult, if not impossible, to accept. I reiterate: the boomers are different. Conscious outreach to baby boomers can be a double-edged sword. Until critical numbers are achieved, overt (and covert) resistance may come from the older membership.

It's Not Just a Generation Gap

The worldview of those born after 1947 is substantially different from the worldview of those born before that date. This difference is profound and cannot be attributed simply to a generation gap.

The events that shaped the expectations of those born before 1947 were the Great Depression and World War II. The events that shaped the lives of those born after 1947 were the war in Vietnam, Watergate, and the women's movement.

Baby boomers have a distinctive historical-social consciousness. This consciousness developed in response to key events that took place during the time in which most of the boomers were in their late adolescence or early adulthood. That period includes the decades from 1960 to 1980.

This radically different worldview has a direct impact on every institution with which the boomers come in contact, including the workplace, home and family, and church. Boomers *are* different. They relate to their world differently. The importance of this fact alone cannot be overemphasized in any discussion of church outreach to members of the boomer generation. The institutional style and worship format that worked well to draw young families to Unitarian Universalist congregations in the 1960s and 1970s will not meet the needs of the boomers. It is important for ministers and membership committees to understand why this is so.

Affluence and Upheaval

Baby boomers came of age in a time unlike any other. The period from 1960 may be characterized by two words: affluence and upheaval. The 1950s and 1960s were a period of unprecedented economic growth, prosperity, and optimism. Children reared during this time grew up not only with great expectations but also with a sense of personal entitlement.

Boomers grew up not just hoping or praying to receive a higher education, or to obtain an interesting, well-paying job, or to enjoy the benefits of a satisfying marriage to a sexy mate, they felt automatically entitled to these opportunities and benefits. The good life was their birthright. The emphasis on individualism, freedom of choice, and personal fulfillment had never been greater.

Whereas those born before 1947 accepted the fact that the external characteristics of race, gender, class, and social role would be the factors that shaped their lives, those born after 1947 expected their destinies to be guided and shaped primarily by their own inner needs and desires.

Likewise, the ethics of self-denial and self-sacrifice that had characterized the lives of the boomer's depression era parents were giving way to the new ethic of self-fulfillment. The primary locus of authority had shifted dramatically from the outer world to the inner world. Their parents were motivated by a sense of duty and loyalty: duty and loyalty to one's country, community, church, job, and family. Boomers are motivated by a sense of duty and loyalty to the self alone.

Pollster Daniel Yankelovich described these changes in his book *New Rules: Searching for Self-Fulfillment in a World Turned Upside Down*, "Instead of asking, 'Will I be able to make a good living?' 'Will I be successful?,' 'Will I raise happy, healthy, successful children?'—the typical questions asked by average Americans in the 1950s and 1960s—Americans in the 1970s came to ponder more introspective matters.

"We asked 'How can I find self-fulfillment?' 'What does personal success really mean?' 'What kinds of commitments should I be making?' 'What is worth sacrificing for?' 'How can I grow?'"

Whether they viewed it as a healthy form of introspection or an unhealthy form of self absorption, because of the emphasis on self-actualization and individual potential that seemed to dominate the imagination of the decade, social critics were quick to label the 1970s as the "Me Decade."

But Yankelovich adds that by the early 1980s another radical change was taking place in the realm of values and priorities. He asserts that among the boomers the ethic of self-fulfillment was gradually giving way to a new ethic of commitment.

Unlike the ethic of self-denial that had characterized their parents or the ethic of self-fulfillment that had characterized the "Me Decade," the new ethic of commitment was directed toward closer and deeper personal relationships. Additionally, another major change was occurring as boomers began to turn from instrumental values to sacred/expressive values.

In summary, the climate of prosperity and economic security in the 1950s and 1960s inverted the hierarchy of values away from the basic needs—survival and economic security—toward the values of individual well-being, personal fulfillment, and greater intellectual and spiritual growth. But by the mid-1980s, boomers were becoming less satisfied with all of this emphasis on the self and were beginning to speak of building community and renewing emotional and spiritual connections to friends, family, the earth, and to God.

Baby Boomers

Personal growth, especially spiritual growth, was still a high priority; individualism and freedom of choice were still very important, but baby boomers were beginning to look for new ways to find self-fulfillment through deeper connections and renewed commitments.

A complete "silent" revolution of values had taken place in less than a generation. But the kind of revolution that most of us associate with the 1960s through 1970s was far from the silent kind. It was a revolution that took place in the streets as well as in bedrooms and boardrooms all across America. This kind of revolution also had a major impact on the lives, attitudes, and commitments of the boomer generation.

The civil rights movement during the 1950s and 1960s, the anti-Vietnam War protests in the 1960s and early 1970s, the women's movement, the gay and lesbian liberation movements radicalized a whole generation of Americans. Idealistic young Americans saw clearly the discrepancy between their nation's professed egalitarian values and the overt and covert methods of racial and sexual discrimination that were woven into the very fabric of American life. The assassinations of John and Robert Kennedy, Martin Luther King, Jr., and Malcolm X. and the Watergate scandal left baby boomers with a further sense of disillusionment as well as a fear and distrust of institutions. The women's movement and the sexual revolution challenged traditional gender roles. Race, class, gender, sexuality, spirituality: Everything was suddenly "up for grabs."

Women and homosexuals adopted the confrontation-style rhetoric and strategies of the civil rights movement in order to gain access to the goods and services that they had been denied. Greater sexual freedom and recreational drug use were accepted as part of the new morality. Abortion on demand evolved from a secret shame to a woman's right to choose.

In the 1960s, two wars were going on that were literally tearing America apart: the war overseas in Vietnam and the values war at home. Although these events were unquestionably the factors that shaped the baby boomer's distinctive historical/social consciousness, exactly how these events affected individual boomers depended largely on whether they were part of the first wave or the second wave of the baby boom.

"First wavers," as those who were born between 1947 and 1954 are called, came of age right in the midst of the most turbulent events of the 1960s. According to Annie Gottlieb in her book *Do You Believe in Magic*, "This first wave was at the epicenter of the cultural earthquake. People now in their mid to late forties met the sixties tide at its flood in their late teens and early twenties. They took the sixties most seriously and were the most traumatized and transformed. First wave people still tend to be earnest, passionate, visionary, and somewhat shell shocked."

According to Wade Clark Roof in his extensive analysis of the boomers, *A Generation of Seekers: The Spiritual Journeys of the Baby Boom Generation*, "Older boomers were the most affected: They had grown up with more confidence in the country than had the younger boomers. They had farther to fall in their disillusionment. Many have yet to regain confidence in this country and its leadership."

"Second wavers," those born after 1954, came of age at the point when the counterculture was beginning to become institutionalized. According to Gottlieb, second wavers "have achieved an easier blend of pragmatism and idealism than their elders. Many cut their hair and got back on the straight track sooner and with less conflict than their older siblings did. Second wavers seem ironic and low key, with lower expectations, and more resiliency."

But both first- and second-wave baby boomers have more in common with each other than with either of the generations that came before or after them. According to a 1985 Gallup poll, both first- and second-wave baby boomers are the least trusting of all age groups toward social and political institutions. A sense of alienation and estrangement born out of their experiences in the turbulent 1960s continue to express themselves as a generalized distrust of government, of major institutions, and of leaders.

Baby Boomers

Compared with other generations, this distrust runs deeper and manifests itself in several different ways. Boomers are less likely to remain loyal to a political party and more likely to vote against an incumbent. They are less likely than their parents to belong to a social organization concerned with community welfare. When buying a product, they are less likely to remain loyal to a single company or brand name. Likewise, when it comes to church affiliation, boomers are shoppers. They have no denominational loyalty, and they make their church shopping decisions quickly and on the basis of first impressions.

Boomers bore the brunt of an additional kind of upheaval and disillusionment as well. Reared during a time of unprecedented economic prosperity and affluence, boomers shared the expectation that they would not only do as well financially as their parents had, but that they would do much better. The economic bust of the 1970s left many boomers with frustrated dreams and diminishing expectations. Boomers might well be referred to as The Disappointed Generation.

In summary: The baby boomers, whose childhoods were characterized by affluence and high expectations, came of age during one of the most tumultuous periods in American history. The boomers suffered from a deep disillusionment brought about by the Vietnam War and Watergate. Their sense of the presence of injustice was increased by the consciousness raising achieved by African Americans, Native Americans, women, homosexuals, and the disabled. Their sense of frustration was increased by economic conditions that kept many boomers from achieving the same standard of living that their parents had enjoyed. Boomers today are haunted by the realistic fear of downward mobility.

Many boomers, especially women, are additionally frustrated and angered by the demands of their careers, the needs of their children, and the increasing dependency of their own aging parents. They call themselves the "Sandwich Generation," caught as they are between two other generations who need their care and attention. Many do not have time to do the volunteer work or to pursue other forms of self-enrichment that they had hoped to do. Most women complain that the burden of "making a home" and nurturing the young still falls primarily on their shoulders.

Baby Boomers and Religion

No generation was more "churched" than the baby boomers, and no generation abandoned organized religion in greater numbers. Nine out of ten baby boomers attended church or synagogue on at least a weekly basis during their childhoods. In their late teen and young adult years, over sixty percent of the boomers became church/synagogue dropouts. Their reasons for abandoning organized religion included disillusionment when their religious communities failed to take a more proactive stance on civil rights or against the Vietnam War and/or frustration over issues such as birth control, abortion, and women's ordination.

Some women as well as some homosexuals left the church because they felt overlooked, condemned, or just shut out of the church power structure. Most of the church/synagogue dropouts left because they found organized religion boring or irrelevant. Twenty years later, although forty-two percent of those who dropped out of church/synagogue show no signs of returning, twenty-five percent of the 78 million baby boomers are starting to return to organized religion.

The majority of boomers who are returning to church say that they are doing so in order to provide religious education and affiliation for their children. This is true. But for those UU ministers and laypersons who will listen with their hearts, what the baby boomers are not saying about their reasons for returning to church are perhaps even more important than their stated reasons. They seek religious education for their children, but they seek solace for themselves as well. What the boomers are not saying is that many boomer families are in pain, if not in crisis, and that they are returning to church because they are seeking to shore up weak or troubled relationships between parents, children, and stepchildren. The boomers are in crisis. And they need what the best of our congregations have to offer.

Other reasons why boomers are returning to church include the search for meaning, the need to experience spiritual renewal, and the desire to find answers to questions concerning suffering and death. Another cluster of reasons boomers are returning to church is a longing for community and the need for a sense of connectedness to something larger than themselves.

As a parish minister, I begin with the assumption that all baby boomer newcomers to my church are in some stage of crisis, whether a family crisis such as a death, a divorce or a major move; a mid-life crisis such as unemployment or illness; a crisis involving alcoholism or drug addiction; or a crisis involving the competing demands of children and career.

For many boomers, belonging is more important than believing, and when they go looking for a religious home, the perceived quality of community life is more important to them than doctrine or denomination. When it comes to looking for a religious home, boomers are shoppers. In 1954 only four percent of churchgoers were attending a church different from the one in which they were raised; today forty-four percent of churchgoers attend a different church than they attended when they were children. Denominational loyalty means little or nothing to them.

They go where they discover the best match between their personal needs and the ability of the religious community to meet those needs.

What Does All of This Mean for Your Church?

Newsweek magazine dubbed Unitarian Universalism the quintessential baby boomer church. Why? Because our emphasis on the individual as the principal locus of religious authority, our lack of dogma, our pluralistic approach to spirituality, and our egalitarianism seem to be in line with existing baby boomer values. Additionally, aspects that attract boomers to Unitarian Universalism include our openness to theological as well as social issues of concern to women as well as gay men and lesbians.

Although we may be the quintessential baby boomer church, the potential for a greater influx of boomers in our congregations is a double-edged sword. The presence of a greater number of boomers can be both a boon to growth and a threat to those church members who were born before 1947.

In the small- to medium-sized congregation, church growth itself may be a source of discomfort for members born before 1947. Many of those persons grew up in a small town and attended a small elementary school (or perhaps even a one-room schoolhouse). They were acculturated to the small group and feel intimidated by larger, more impersonal institutions.

According to church growth consultant Herb Miller, as many as twenty percent of these persons feel emotionally uncomfortable in groups larger than 100. Older members will begin to say things like, "I used to know everyone's name here. Who are these new people?" What they really mean is, "Everyone here used to know my name and recognize how important I've been to this congregation over the years. These new people aren't demonstrating a proper respect for my opinions and contributions."

In contrast, many baby boomers attended larger, overcrowded public schools in the 1960s and 1970s and feel comfortable in a larger group—and in fact seek out larger groups for the variety of activities and relationships they offer. They are more "turned on" by a larger group with a variety of small subgroups that they may join or not join as they please.

To reemphasize the point: It is not the proverbial generation gap that separates baby boomers from their parents or older siblings. When boomers encounter persons who were born before 1947, two radically different worldviews collide. This collision of worldviews can undermine church growth strategies and set up a conflict between the loyal old-timers, who have given much to the institution, and the newcomers with their blatant consumer orientation unless this potential conflict is understood and skillfully addressed by church leadership.

Baby Boomers

Although it may be a bit of an overgeneralization, the majority of UUs born before 1947 tend to be "come outers," those who left a church of another denomination for intellectual or ideological reasons. They came to Unitarian Universalism seeking freedom of religion and in some cases, freedom from religion. Although these persons bring with them a wealth of good institutional experience and expertise, they may have an almost knee-jerk reaction against what they call "God talk," emotionalism, ritual, and formalism.

The majority of baby boomer UUs are "come inners," those who, although they might have been exposed to church and Sunday school as young children, were virtually unchurched as adults. Boomers are seeking spiritual nurture and direction. Their tastes are wide ranging and eclectic and embrace both traditional religious symbols as well as New Age philosophies. Whereas the boomers do not have the automatic resistance to those words and rituals that the "come outers" react against, they lack the institutional experience and expertise that the "come outers" brought with them to Unitarian Universalism.

Conflict Over the Sunday Worship Service

Sunday morning worship is this first place where a conflict of values between those born before 1947 and the boomers is likely to occur in a UU congregation. Sunday morning has the potential to turn into a showdown between oldtimers and newcomers, or it can turn into a major opportunity for growth. A growing congregation must approach this potential source of conflict with eyes wide open.

Intellectual stimulation on Sunday morning is desired most by church members born before 1947. They prefer sermons that deal with ideas, concepts, and issues. They are comfortable with a style of presentation that is objective, detached, and emotionally neutral.

Celebration and spiritual renewal is number one among baby boomers. They prefer sermons that deal with feelings, personal dilemmas, life passages, and spiritual growth. They are comfortable with a style of sermon presentation that is subjective, personal, warm, and vibrant.

Those born before 1947 associate the words "celebration" and "spiritual renewal" with emotionalism. And they are the ones most likely to say that they do not like religious services that contain "emotionalism." In contrast, those UUs born after 1947 say that they do not like Sunday services that are dry, boring, cold, and feel too much like a college lecture.

The language of worship may be a problem as well. Those born before 1947 often react negatively to what they perceive as "God talk"—theistic language or metaphoric language in the worship service. Change the liturgical language and they are apt to say: "If we wanted to hear this kind of talk, we'd have never left the Methodist Church!"

Women born after 1947 often react very negatively to what they call "man talk," the use of the noun "man," as in mankind, man-made, manpower, chairman, in lieu of more gender-neutral words, such as human being or humankind, person power, and chairperson. Additionally some women, influenced by feminist theology, prefer the term Goddess to God, or insist that those terms be used together or interchangeably. Many boomer women who call themselves radical feminists say that they crave more ritualized and participatory worship and less lecture-style worship.

Children in the worship service can also be an issue that divides older members from boomers. Baby boomers, many of whom are seeking a church in which their children are also welcome, are comfortable with the presence of children in all or part of the worship service. Those born before 1947 often find children in the service a distraction.

UUs born before 1947 prefer, or are at least have grown accustomed to, a style of worship that is informal, loosely structured, nonliturgical, and oftentimes lay led. Those born after 1947 prefer a worship service that is fast paced, tightly form atted, and professionally led. They are even comfortable with more liturgical forms of worship that they refer to as *ritual*.

Baby Boomers

Those born before 1947 prefer Sunday music to be classical and meditative. Recorded music suits them fine, whereas those born after 1947 prefer Sunday music to be modern, singable, up tempo, and live.

Sermons that resonate with first-wave baby boomers evoke the best of the images and ideals that characterized the great social movements of the 1960s. The rhetoric of John Kennedy and Martin Luther King, Jr., the risks and rewards of the Freedom Riders, the volunteer spirit of the Peace Corps and VISTA, the feelings of comradery, solidarity, and optimism that existed among college-aged men and women during that period, speak to the longings of men and women now approaching their fifties.

Sermons that speak to members of the second wave of the boom are more introspective and focus on issues of personal growth and healing, as well as psychological and spiritual insight. The writings of M. Scott Peck, Anne Wilson Schaef, Matthew Fox, and Starhawk and the language of the addiction/recovery movement speak to the needs of those members of the boom who are just turning forty. Second-wave baby boomers are skeptical, yet vulnerable. They long to experience real commitment, whether to another person, a cause, or an institution.

The keys to attracting and holding baby boomers in worship services are these: a fast-paced service that starts strong and maintains a good momentum. Good, live, singable music is not just a plus, it is a must. Children should be included in all or part of the service. Sermon topics should deal with personal growth issues, ethical dilemmas, rites of passage, and classical religious topics, such as guilt and grace. Meaningful rituals, especially those that include children, are critical. And last, but not least, the service should *feel* like a worship service, not a town meeting or a college lecture. Sermon "talk backs" are not as big a "draw" for boomers as they are for those members born before 1947.

Although the conflict over the style and content of your Sunday worship service may be couched in terms of the classic theism versus humanism debate, today it is a conflict that has less to do with theology and more to do with the experiences, needs, and expectations of two very different generations. Some growing congregations with significant numbers of boomers as well as persons born before 1947 might consider two Sunday morning services with slightly different formats.

Conflict Over Duty Versus Fulfillment

Sunday worship is not the only aspect of church life in which those born before 1947 may come into conflict with baby boomers. Volunteerism and fundraising are two other areas in which the differing styles of these two generations seem to collide.

Those persons who came of age during the Great Depression and World War II have a finely honed sense of duty, obligation, institutional loyalty, and a willingness to make personal sacrifices for the common good. When approaching members of this generation for donations of their time and/or money, the most successful appeals draw on these characteristics.

When approaching baby boomers, however, the most successful appeals tap into their desires for personal fulfillment and a sense of community. An opportunity for creativity, personal expression, and fellowship must be built into volunteer jobs if you wish to recruit boomers.

For example, a church member born before 1947 will couch an every-member canvass appeal in images and language that evoke a sense of duty to the church. "Where would we all be if it were not for Old First Church? We will all have to pull together again this year and make a sacrifice to keep it running. If we don't do it, nobody else will. If you don't make your pledge, we won't be able to pay the bills."

This kind of language falls flat with baby boomers. They have a consumer orientation, and they are only willing to give time and money to a successful institution that will benefit them in the long run. A canvass appeal couched in the language of desperation and need will send boomers packing. A canvass appeal designed to reach baby boomers might say: "Join together to make our growing church community even more vibrant and alive. This is your chance to be part of something really special: a growing church with even more programs to meet the needs of you and your family."

A wise canvass committee will couch their annual appeal in ways that speak to the needs of those born before 1947 as well as those born after 1947.

Conclusion

Unitarian Universalism has an unprecedented opportunity for growth. Many of the experiences and values that make the baby boomer generation unique also predispose them to the good news of liberal religion. However, previous generations of Unitarian Universalists may find it difficult to adjust to the changes that the boomers will bring with them.

Church growth may bring with it unanticipated conflict in the areas of worship, volunteerism, and fundraising. Leaders need to understand how and why the baby boomers are different and consciously determine how the individual churches can reach out to the boomers without alienating their existing membership.

Church growth consultant Herb Miller suggests that although the churches must make reaching a new generation of adults a high priority, church leaders should give that goal less overt publicity than the goal of caring for our present membership. You don't want to make your long-time members feel that their needs and likes will be ignored in an effort to win boomers.

Those who were born before 1947 bring some very special gifts to their church. Not the least of these are institutional savvy and an unshakable loyalty to the institution. And Lord knows, they've paid some dues. But baby boomers bring with them a certain vitality, a commitment to social justice and spiritual renewal that has been lacking for a long time in Unitarian Universalism. We need both kinds of gifts. And with faith and skill we will grow and succeed.

Counting the Ways to 250,000 by 2001

Charles A. Gaines

SEVERAL YEARS AGO, I attempted to express my vision for the Unitarian Universalist Association. In a report to the Board of Trustees, I made a provocative statement. In one sound bite, I said that I would like to have "250,000 Unitarian Universalists by 2001." Since I made that statement, many have rallied to express the same call. Formerly we used words such as "anticlericalism," "the fellowship movement," and "anything goes." These words are now considered "out." Today the "in" words are "evangelism," "growth," "professional leadership," and "mission." Evangelism, growth, and professional leadership will lead us to a membership of 250,000. Of course, we all know that it isn't really the numbers that matter. It is what numbers can do.

In 1826, Harriet Beecher Stowe moved with her family to Boston. Her father was an orthodox minister. Stowe described a scene different from the one her father espoused: "All the literary men of Massachusetts were Unitarian. All the trustees and professors of Harvard College were Unitarians. All the elite of wealth and fashion crowded Unitarian churches. The judges on the bench were Unitarians."

250,000 by 2001

Even beyond Boston, Unitarianism was a force in society. The Whig Party with Daniel Webster, John Quincy Adams, and Millard Fillmore, all Unitarians, espoused Unitarian principles of economic progress and freedom from tyranny. Before the Civil War, John C. Calhoun and Jefferson C. Davis—both Unitarians—were espousing similar beliefs from the Southern perspective.

Even more important than the political was the cultural dominance of Unitarians. Illustrious persons such as Ralph Waldo Emerson, Henry David Thoreau, William Cullen Bryant, Oliver Wendell Holmes, Sr., James Russell Lowell, Louisa May Alcott, Nathaniel Hawthorne, Edgar Allen Poe, and Henry Wordsworth Longfellow were all Unitarians—and household names throughout nineteenth-century America.

The Universalists have an equally exciting story. In 1840, Universalists were found in every state and territory of the nation—with 700 societies and 311 preachers. In the twelve years that followed, their numbers doubled, so that by 1852 some have estimated, there were over a half-million Universalists in America.

More than a century later, we see that neither our numbers nor our influence has lasted. There are some Unitarian Universalists who don't think influence and numbers matter. Such persons prefer the position stated by William Ellery Channing, a leading minister of early American Unitarianism, when he referred to efforts to multiply to be expressions of "the guilt of the sectarian spirit."

I, myself, prefer the naiveté of Thomas Jefferson when he predicted that before he died everyone would be a Unitarian. As Unitarian Universalists, we have been somehow conditioned to disavow the importance of numbers. "The Catholics, Baptists, Mormons, and others have the numbers. We have the quality," is how our thinking sometimes goes. We often dismiss any counting exercise as trivial. When we moan and groan about the state of the world or of New York City, and do nothing to implement our ideals, that is, communicating our faith and increasing our numbers, we agree with Oliver Cromwell when he said, "a few honest men are better than numbers." But Oliver Cromwell's actions spoke louder than his words. Despite the discomfort many Unitarian Universalists have with numbers, I believe that our numbers will be a powerful resource, that numbers will help us have a hand in shaping the future.

Numbers win elections. Representatives who either serve our values and affirm our perspectives—or representatives who serve larger constituencies that oppose much of what we believe in—are selected through a process of counting numbers. Anyone who reads the morning newspaper and criticizes what they see happening in the State House or in our nation's Capitol cannot belittle the idea that more people need exposure to Unitarian Universalism. We need more governors in state houses, more legislators in Washington, and more judges on the benches who represent the ideals and principles of Unitarian Universalism. We need more people thinking about saving our environment, guaranteeing individual free choice, promoting justice and compassion. We need more people working in those areas where the disenfranchised, the homeless, and abused women and children dwell. We need more people speaking our values and voting for the persons who will translate Unitarian Universalist principles into concrete proposals for a better world. All this is what might be meant by the word "salvation." Salvation is what we all want in this world—and it is the kind of salvation that has a great deal to do with numbers.

Numbers help us take the temperature of how we are doing in our home congregations and as a denomination. Numbers are the tangible expression of health and vitality. We may choose to resist or ignore this idea, but beyond our own frame of reference, numbers tell us something about trends and can predict where we are likely to head in the future.

A congregation that experiences a ten to twenty percent loss in membership over a period of five years should take a serious look at numbers. A congregation in which the Sunday attendance is gradually falling each year should see what such numbers mean. This is especially important if the church school enrollment is also declining. Counting the house is a way of taking our temperature. The results cannot be explained away.

Counting the number of in-area visitors who come to our churches during the week is a significant exercise. A congregation that holds worship services each week but has fewer visitors over a period of eighteen months to two years than their total membership should take serious note of these numbers also. Such a congregation should consider ways of becoming better known in the community and devise new programs and ministries that truly mesh with the needs of people in the area.

A congregation that has many visitors—but few joining or returning to the congregation—should take a serious look at the record, and should look for what meaning the numbers imply. Such congregations might interview some of these visitors who do not return. It is always more comforting to interview those who join the congregation. Frequent visitors or new members will most likely tell the story one wants to hear. By talking with those who do not return, we may learn some things about our welcoming process and our programs.

A congregation that loses almost as many members as it gains over a period of two to five years should seriously assess the meaning of these numbers. Such congregations often have subtle and not-so-subtle barriers for newcomer involvement. Sometimes, those in power don't want to let go. Other times, there are too few programs offering opportunities for the quality involvement newcomers expect. Responses such as "we tried that once," "we can't afford it," or "they won't like it," stifles newcomer initiative and enthusiasm.

Counting the average age of your membership and comparing the present average age to what the average age was five or ten years ago is another numbers exercise that can predict your future. The average congregation has a lifetime of twenty-five years. Unless a new generation takes up the banner, the congregation will decline and eventually die. No congregation should wait until the average age is above fifty-five years of age. Strategic long-range planning based on a vision/mission orientation is one way to respond to a "growing older" congregation.

Another numbers exercise is assessing the total income of all the members and other participants in your congregation. Calculating your total pledges in comparison to the congregation's total income may show a dearth of generous commitment. Congregations in which the vision/mission is high or those that are expanding their facilities through an ambitious building program frequently report total pledges in the neighborhood of three to five percent of total member income. A response from many Unitarian Universalists to this kind of commitment is that their own congregation is different from those reporting three to five percent of income pledges. A frequent response is that their congregation is made up of people with low incomes. The retired often say this, even though many members have total estate portfolios that far exceed the national portfolio average.

All of the above says something about numbers. Numbers can help to destroy and to save our world. Numbers help to tell us how we are doing as individual congregations and as a denomination. No matter how one defines quality programming, spiritual growth, excellence in ministry, competent lay leadership, friendly atmosphere, or relevance, lining up our words with our actions is the bottom line. The bottom line is numerical.

That's why I like daring Unitarian Universalists to enter the future in droves. I like the biting sound of 250,000 Unitarian Universalists by 2001. Whether this goal is illusive or realistic depends on us. We chart the course to achievement when we analyze the simple and specific data compiled in our congregations—when we pay attention to the numbers.

The fact of the matter is that no single person or congregation, nor the entire staff of the UUA, nor the professional district staff alone enables significant membership growth. Growth is the symphony of us all working together. If each congregation, with a core of committed individuals, performs and analyzes the specific data of the various counting exercises and takes the necessary measures that will promote or change the direction of evidencing trends, then in a new spirit of interdependence all of us together can evolve toward a greater and better future. The future I envision is one in which each Unitarian Universalist experiences connection to every other Unitarian Universalist in their congregation, each congregation senses its connection to every other congregation in the Unitarian Universalist Association, and the Unitarian Universalist Association experiences itself linked to other Unitarians and Universalists throughout the world. In the spirit of our deepest commitment, we will all feel linked in the family of humankind. It is the spirit of all of us being in this together that brings not only our own but our world's salvation.

How Sweet the Sound

*The Role of Music in
Unitarian Universalist
Evangelism*

John E. Giles

ALMOST EVERYONE KNOWS that music packs a tremendous emotional wallop. Successful movie moguls, advertising executives, and army generals all realize that music's impact is not limited to opera, ballet, and Broadway musicals. Think for a moment of the opening credits to the movie *Star Wars*; without the soundtrack, the opening shots of outer space would be rather dull, but when John Williams's thrilling score is added, the audience knows that an exciting adventure is about to unfold. Advertising jingles like "Winston tastes good like a (click! click!) cigarette should" not only help the consumer remember the name of a product long after the advertising campaign is over, but can make even the most harmful products seem innocuous.

And, of course, virtually every country in history has sent its young men and women off to war with stirring marches and rousing songs that promise personal glory and easy victory. During the Vietnam War, the US Defense Department spent millions of dollars on army and navy bands which played John

The Role of Music

Philip Sousa marches and other patriotic tunes, while the war protesters countered by singing Pete Seeger's "Where Have All the Flowers Gone?" and listening to acid rock.

The most potent demonstrations of music's raw, even frightening power arise when the forces of justice confront the tools of oppression. The story of music's role in the March on Selma, Alabama, is often told. As the people who were protesting the city's segregation laws approached the bridge outside the town, they could not help but notice the thousands of well-armed state troopers and militia who stood on the opposite side of the bridge, waiting to prevent them from entering Selma. For a long time the unarmed protesters warily eyed the guns, the clubs, and the dogs on the other side of the bridge; for many minutes they were afraid to move despite the urging of their leaders to do so. Finally, one old woman began singing the simple hymn that Dr. Martin Luther King once described as "the most powerful tool of the Civil Rights movement," "We Shall Overcome." Only after the throng had joined the old woman on the verse "We are not afraid" did they find the courage to walk across the bridge. More than one state trooper remarked after the incident that the unnerving prospect of killing thousands of people singing "We Shall Overcome" was probably the single most important reason that they did not fire on the protesters.

The unmistakable power of music has also been harnessed by the world's many religions. One need only hear a few seconds of the Islamic "call to prayer" or a few measures of an old Shaker tune in order to recognize the religion involved. The psalms of a Jewish cantor or the chants of a Roman Catholic priest are as integral to those religions as reading the Torah or celebrating the Eucharist. It is difficult to imagine the Mormons without their famous Tabernacle Choir or the Salvation Army without its brass bands.

Moreover, the ability of music to mold and influence the human spirit has not been lost on our fundamentalist and conservative counterparts on the other side of the culture wars. Because children are particularly susceptible to music's beguiling charms, our fundamentalist friends lavish their children's music programs with huge amounts of energy, time, *and money*.

I personally witnessed the effects of such musical indoctrination when a dear friend, who is *not* a musician, visited me in my home with her two young children. Because she knows that I am a musician, she asked her children what song they would like to perform for me. The children excitedly chose to sing their very favorite song, a hymn they called the "Thunder Alleluia" (set to the tune of "Hyfrydol"):

> Alleluia! sing to Jesus! his the scepter, his the throne!
> Alleluia! his the triumph, his the victory alone;
> Hark! the songs of peaceful Zion *thunder* like a mighty
> flood;
> Jesus out of every nation hath redeemed us by his blood.

Their performance may not have equaled the Vienna Boys' Choir for musical artistry, but the love that passed between the mother and her children as they enthusiastically sang this exclusive, patriarchal hymn was extraordinary. As they "basked in the glow of Jesus" (their mother's description of singing as a family), I could not help but think that when these children become adults, they will probably embrace the hymn's masculine, hierarchical images of God, just as their mother embraced them as they witnessed for their faith in the apartment of a Unitarian Universalist. And, I also wondered, how many Unitarian Universalist moms (or dads) take the time to teach their children songs from our liberal religious tradition?

Our conservative religious colleagues also appreciate the importance of music in the spiritual lives of their adult parishioners. The senior minister of a particularly vibrant fundamentalist congregation (whose 10,000 members are all required to give one-tenth of their gross income to the church) was once asked, "If you had to cut your support staff from twelve full-time ministers to one, which person would you retain?" His answer was swift and simple: "I would keep my minister of music; she brings in more people to this church than all the other ministers combined."

The fundamentalists' commitment to music even extends to the architecture of their churches. It is now common for them to build the choral rehearsal room next to the sanctuary, so that the choir has easy access to the choir loft after it robes each Sunday. When I asked one conservative pastor why he so willingly gave up the traditional prestigious spot adjoining the sanctuary to the choir, he responded, "I am only one person. Our adult choir has over sixty people; our children's choirs and instrumental ensembles involve at least three hundred more people. By placing the musicians' space next to the sanctuary, we acknowledge the indispensable role they play in the life of our growing congregation." I could not help but contrast his words with the reaction of one lifelong Unitarian Universalist activist who, during her visits to over one hundred Unitarian Universalist churches, had never even heard of the *concept* of a separate choral rehearsal space, much less seen one placed next to a sanctuary.

Unfortunately, we Unitarian Universalists, with our rich heritage of brilliant preachers who stress rational thought, religious tolerance, and commitment to social action, have seldom placed a high priority on music. Our actions bespeak our priorities: The Unitarian Universalist Association does not yet have an office for music, our seminaries do not offer a single course on music, and our professional musicians are often paid less than our janitors.

Even more importantly, we Unitarian Universalists do not yet have a strong tradition of our own, uniquely Unitarian Universalist music. Because American Unitarianism and Universalism evolved from northern European Protestant traditions, it was natural for our overworked ministers to do what they did best: adapt the old worship traditions in a way that made sense for the emerging religious liberals of their time. In the musical realm, this meant writing new texts to familiar English and German Protestant tunes. Thus, "Onward Christian

Soldiers" became "Forward through the Ages" and "Jesus Christ Is Risen Today" became "Lo, the Earth Awakes Again." Even the great nineteenth-century Universalist hymn sings at Murray Grove, New Jersey, where "the fervent singing could be heard for miles around" used traditional Christian tunes to accompany the newly penned liberal lyrics. Only occasionally did a Unitarian or Universalist text get paired with a *new* tune that entered the wider culture: "It Came Upon a Midnight Clear"; "Once to Every Man and Nation" (which is now considered so controversial that it has been dropped even from most liberal Christian hymnals); "I Heard the Bells on Christmas Day" (which is still looking for an appropriate tune); "Battle Hymn of the Republic" (which is now considered too controversial for the UU hymnal); and the ubiquitous "Jingle Bells." And even the new tunes which accompanied the Unitarian or Universalist texts, with the exception of *Jingle Bells*, sounded so much like their Protestant counterparts that they were virtually indistinguishable from the hymns used by Presbyterians or Methodists.

This tradition of adapting music from other religious cultures continued into the second half of the twentieth century when Unitarian Universalists began dabbling in music that originated outside northern Europe. Jewish hymns that celebrated Yom Kippur, Hanukkah, and Passover found their way into our services, as did spirituals and other tunes from the African American gospel tradition. (Once again, word changes were made: "We Are Climbing Jacob's Ladder" became "We Are Dancing Sarah's Circle.") Some Unitarian Universalist musicians began using music from the popular culture during worship; the most often sung hymn in Unitarian Universalist churches, "Morning Has Broken," languished unused in our hymnal until the British rock star Cat Stevens "introduced" it to the world in 1971. Others began using guitars and up-tempo keyboard styles to introduce protest songs from the civil rights and labor movements to our congregations. The most avant-garde Unitarian Universalist musicians even included music from the Orient, native American cultures, and the Broadway stage in our worship services. But as exciting as these innovations proved to be, they nevertheless retained the old Unitarian Universalist habit of borrowing music from another culture or religious heritage, rather than creating a musical style unique to Unitarian Universalists.

The problem with using the music of other religions, even those songs made popular by rock stars, was that the music inevitably evoked memories of the original context. This paradox was often the source of humor for April Fool's Day services, when hymns like "Holy, Holy, Holy, Lord God Almighty" were parodied as "Coffee, Coffee, Coffee, All We Want Is Coffee." But beneath all the light-hearted frivolity simmered a faint, uneasy suspicion that we Unitarian Universalists lacked a musical tradition that expressed our spirituality in a deeply emotional way.

Fortunately, a growing band of Unitarian Universalist hymn writers has been addressing this problem in recent years by composing tunes and texts that embody our ideals and express our beliefs. Because most of these artists are both poets and composers, they have fashioned new creations that so inextricably intertwine music and poetry that it is hard to imagine one without the other. Their poetry takes, *as its starting point*, such Unitarian Universalist concepts as gender inclusiveness, universal images of transcending love, and respect for the interdependent web of all existence. Gone are those awkward passages where a recently written gender-inclusive word or phrase calls attention to itself by reminding the parishioner of the nonacceptable original. Gone are the poems whose imagery, no matter how theologically correct, is too prosaic to displace the memory of the text traditionally associated with a particular tune.

By the same token, although these creations use various elements of jazz, blues, gospel, spirituals, pop, new age music, and even traditional hymnody, they copy no single musical style. Indeed, I am reluctant to call these works "hymns," because to do so would imply a stodginess they do not exhibit. Rather, these uniquely Unitarian Universalist creations offer both a musical style so fresh that it successfully avoids reminding anyone of another religious heritage and a poetic palette that honestly reflects our theological perspective.

I first became aware of the fierce pride that Unitarian Universalists are taking in these new hymns during the centennial celebration of the Parliament of World Religions, held in Chicago during September 1993. Part of the opening plenary session was devoted to hearing brief musical examples which celebrated the various religious heritages of the participants. Roman Catholicism, Eastern Orthodoxy, Islam, Judaism, Hinduism, Buddhism, Lutheranism, and even Native American sects each rendered beautiful, painstakingly prepared musical selections that witnessed to the faith of their adherents. Meanwhile, all the Unitarian Universalists in the audience began wondering how they would be represented on the program, or would they once again be subsumed under the vague rubric of "aberrant Judeo-Christians"?

Finally the Reverend Tony Larsen took the stage and began to sing an unaccompanied hymn from our hymnal, *Singing the Living Tradition*:

> Spirit of Life, come unto me.
> Sing in my heart all the stirrings of compassion.
> Blow in the wind, rise in the sea;
> Move in the hand, giving life the shape of justice.
> Roots hold me close; wings set me free;
> Spirit of Life, come to me, come to me.

While he sang Carolyn McDade's beautiful hymn, the Reverend Larsen also signed it, using the international sign language for the deaf. As his powerful, untrained voice died away at the song's conclusion, hardly a dry eye remained in the house. Certainly the Unitarian Universalists in attendance were deeply moved, for many of us had seldom experienced such a powerful moment of evangelical witness for our religion, a witness heightened by the immediate emotional impact of music.

The gathering of new hymns with music from the Jewish

The Role of Music

("Hevenu Shalom Aleychem"), African-American ("Every Time I Feel the Spirit"), Far Eastern ("Sakura"), and Appalachian Mountain ("Amazing Grace") traditions, as well as old "UU favorites," into a single source results in one of the most effective evangelical tools we Unitarian Universalists possess: our hymnal.

Although hymns are seldom thought of as recruiting devices, they nevertheless remain one of the most effective tools available to evangelistic religious liberals. Because hymns and songs do not require large choirs, expensive organs, or even a building, they can be used just as effectively by the smallest society as by the largest church. Hymns, especially when memorized, are also extremely portable. They can be easily taken to a nursing home, a protest march, a hospital room, a campfire, a basketball court, or a yoga class. Hymns can provide solace when life becomes difficult or tasks grow tedious. One of my earliest memories is of my sixty-year-old babysitter singing "I Walk in the Garden Alone" after her husband was killed in a coal-mining accident. And as we go about our daily lives, hymns can help us recall feelings or ideas that we encountered at church.

Not too long ago I was visiting a friend in the hospital who was facing some very serious surgery. Because I was her Lay Minister of Music, she asked me to sing "Spirit of Life" to help calm her fears. My voice quickly filled the small room and soon began attracting the attention of the hospital staff and patients. And then a most remarkable thing happened: my friend, who was supposed to be too weak to speak, much less sing, surprised us all by adding her clear, steady voice to my rendition.

Everyone was amazed at my friend's transformation; everyone wanted to know the name of the song and where I had found it. When I explained that "Spirit of Life" had appeared in the Unitarian Universalist hymnal, we began a discussion of religion in general and Unitarian Universalism in particular. Because two of the nurses seemed particularly intrigued by a church that had no doctrine, I spent a few additional minutes relating my personal spiritual odyssey with them. The next Sunday I saw them sitting in the congregation. I do not know whether they will eventually join our church or not, but I *do* know that if I had not sung "Spirit of Life" in that hospital room, I would not have found myself talking about Unitarian Universalism with a bunch of strangers!

In order for a hymn to be used as a tool to introduce our ideas to non-Unitarian Universalists, it must not only accurately reflect our theology and be easy to sing, but it must also be familiar enough so that the congregation can perform it enthusiastically. Few things make a visitor squirm as much as a room full of people who are uncomfortable with an emotional force as powerful as music. This "comfort factor" explains my suggestion that a church choose a few of the new "all-UU" hymns (ten at most) and sing them week after week, month after month, until everyone has virtually memorized them. A special hymn can be chosen to accompany particular actions (lighting of the chalice, taking the offering, sending the children to their religious education classes, etc.) that transpire every Sunday. At the Unitarian Church of Evanston, Illinois, we sing "Spirit of Life" each week as the minister finishes his spoken meditation.

Other teaching strategies include rehearsing a new hymn before the service begins, choosing an unfamiliar selection as Hymn of the Month, moving the choir out of the choir loft and into the aisles during hymns to assist the congregation, having the minister encourage the congregation to sing the next verse louder, providing a song leader to teach a new hymn phrase by phrase, and allowing the choir to sing the hymn before the congregation attempts it. But no matter what tactic I use to teach unfamiliar hymns (and I've used them all!), I have found it helpful to inform the congregation of my intent that they *will* sing this new hymn with gusto before the morning is over.

Moreover, the process of learning new hymns does not have to be confined to Sunday morning worship. Hymns can be used to open or close various committee meetings, enliven potluck dinners, complement religious education curricula, and enrich adult programming. Many of the selections in *Singing the Living Tradition* work particularly well at monthly "hootenannies," where the people who love to play guitars, banjos, and other folk instruments can shine. Hymns can be used to help set the mood at the weekly meditation service, the occasional Cakes for the Queen of Heaven class, or the monthly Men's Meeting. An annual hymn sing, which involves everyone in the church from the first grade class to the Swinging Singles group, can help generate excitement for hymns, generate a little extra money (especially if food is served afterward), and provide a "safe" pretext for inviting a friend to church, since no sermons are allowed on Hymn Night. But the bottom line remains the same: the more times a hymn is sung, the more familiar and comfortable it becomes, and the greater the chance that it can be used as a tool for Unitarian Universalist evangelism.

Second only to congregational hymn singing as a musical tool for evangelism is the volunteer choir. Although professional instrumentalists, paid choristers, and music majors from the local university can add immeasurably to a Sunday morning service, there is nothing quite like seeing one's fellow church members working together to create something beautiful during worship. A good choral performance can instill a sense of "church pride" in both the choristers and nonchoristers, just as a winning basketball program can create a "team spirit" for an entire high school, not just the players.

This sense of "church pride" that a successful choral program can bring to a church helps everyone become more effective recruiters for church attendance. Because most of our congregants are not theologians, many people are uncomfortable about discussing religion in the workplace, on the racquetball court, or at the PTA meeting. But if a parishioner honestly thinks the church choir is a cut above the average, it is relatively easy to invite a friend to church by saying, "You should hear our choir sometime; they're really good!"

This scenario is even more compelling for the choir members, because they are able to invite their singing friends to join the choir. One of our recent Board of Trustee Chairs first came to the church thirteen years ago because one of her friends said,

"You will not believe our new choir director: I am singing things I didn't know were possible!" The friend thought she was joining a new choir; instead, she found her spiritual home. Another person who joined our church because she wanted to sing in the choir is currently studying to become a Unitarian Universalist minister at Meadville/Lombard seminary.

Choirs can also act as ambassadors for Unitarian Universalism in other forums beside the church. Some UU choirs perform with local orchestras; some sing the national anthem at major sporting events; some sing on local television shows; others make recordings and sell them in local record stores; still others present an annual "P.D.Q. Bach Night" or madrigal dinner, which can attract a surprisingly wide following in the surrounding community. All of these outside activities, at the very least, put the words "Unitarian Universalist" before the public. And if the choir performs well, the public begins to associate our denomination with beauty, pride, and excellence.

Obviously, large churches with large memberships and large budgets in large cities stand a better chance of fielding "cathedral choirs" than small churches or societies in rural locations. But even the smallest churches usually have a few people who like to sing, and a choir of eight in a church of eighty can generate the same excitement that a choir of eighty can generate in a church of 800. The size of the choir is seldom the issue; after all, even the world's most gifted barbershop quartet only has four members. Nor is the issue architectural limitations; the choirs in many smaller churches sit with their families until it is time to sing the anthem. Then they gather around the piano or next to the flaming chalice, perform their piece, and return to their families.

Rather, the issue usually becomes, How does the choir sound? Because most parishioners do not have the expertise to help a motley crew of amateurs sound like a semiprofessional chorus, it often becomes necessary to add a trained musician to the church's staff. Finding the funds to pay yet another staff person can be a daunting task, but few churches regret having spent the money once they see for themselves how many new members (and pledging units) a good church choir can attract. Indeed, one lifelong Unitarian Universalist recently told me that "taking the time to find the right music director proved as important a decision for our growing congregation as finding the right minister had been."

Church choirs not only act as ambassadors to people outside the church, but they send powerful messages to those inside it as well. To new members, the choir embodies commitment of time and talent to the church. No other single activity at the Unitarian Church of Evanston demands so heavy a time commitment as does membership in the choir: two rehearsals per week, every week for nine months, plus business meetings, special rehearsals, and occasional outside appearances, even "tours." Moreover, most of the choir members serve on other committees and take part in other church activities; eight of the last thirteen chairpersons of our Board of Trustees were choir members. Indeed, choir members tend to be pillars of the church: It is not coincidence that ministers refer to "preaching to the choir," rather than preaching to the budget committee.

To single people, volunteer church choirs send two messages. First, singles are as welcome here as people who are coupled: The choir's purpose is to make music, not introduce spouses. Second, the choir provides a safe place for those who wish to meet and interact with other single people with whom you share at least one mutual interest: making music. As a result, three couples have met in our church choir and eventually married each other, a fact which has immensely helped my recruiting efforts, both inside and outside the congregation. To gay men, lesbians, and bisexuals, church choirs also send the message "you are welcome here," especially in suburban congregations that often focus on religious education and other programs for children and their parents. A chorister need not have children or grandchildren to make music, and in most Unitarian Universalist churches, we occasionally sing about gay issues. Indeed, as the familiar song so aptly puts it, "All

God's creatures got a place in the choir!"

One of the advantages that choirs enjoy over instrumental ensembles is that choral music combines the emotional impact of music with the power of the word. Whether the anthem directly addresses the point of the sermon (my favorite example is performing George Gershwin's "It Ain't Necessarily So" when the minister speaks on "skepticism") or is a "generic UU anthem" (e.g., Randall Thompson's setting of Robert Frost's "The Road Not Taken"), having a text allows the nonmusical or tone-deaf congregant be an equal participant in the musical portions of the service. Matching anthem texts to Unitarian Universalist sermon topics has become somewhat easier in recent years because many members of the Unitarian Universalist Musicians Network (UUMN) have been composing pieces to meet our liberal religious needs, although I have yet to find an appropriate anthem on the subject of abortion. (The readings in *Singing the Living Tradition*, by the way, are a gold mine of possibility for anthem texts.) The need for so many of our members and our visitors to understand and ponder the text has resulted in my belief that the weekly Order of Service should always include the entire text of all choral pieces.

Unfortunately, texted music often raises serious theological questions that instrumental music does not have to address. Seldom have clarinet players or organists ever had to concern themselves with the spiritual appropriateness of their musical renditions. Unitarian Universalist choral directors, however, have found themselves in serious trouble when they have programmed music with patriarchal, racist, or other insensitive texts. One UU music director inadvertently started a huge church fight by continuing the local tradition of performing *Handel's Chorus* on Easter, even after the newly arrived minister had voiced her displeasure with the phrase "the Lord God omnipotent reigneth."

Sometimes substituting a more inclusive phrase for a more exclusive one (e.g., "Let all the world rejoice" instead of "Good Christian men rejoice") can solve the problem, but if the music and its text are extremely familiar, text substitutions often just exacerbate the tension. I have found the UUMN guideline on this subject particularly helpful: avoid insensitive texts whenever possible, but if a compelling reason exists to include a "questionable" piece without word changes, find a worshipful way to explain your choice to the congregation during the service.

The spiritual potential of a strong musical piece coupled with a powerful and appropriate text was dramatically illustrated on Thursday, January 17, 1991, the day after the Gulf War began. A heavy mood hung over our church as the choir gathered for its weekly Thursday night rehearsal; even those members who had not particularly opposed Desert Storm were upset by the instant television coverage of the war's outbreak and the nation's jingoistic reaction to its impersonal, "high-tech" carnage. One chorister finally broke the atypically gloomy spell by suggesting that we sing my choral setting of the Reverend Kenneth G. Hurto's "Were I to Wish You Peace This Evening" just for ourselves:

> Were I to wish you peace this evening,
> I would wish you peace!
> Peace to heal the fragments of our days,
> Peace to renew your spirit,
> Peace to restore your soul,
> Peace which comes from understanding,
> Peace which moves you to unrest
> As long as there is falsehood and injustice,
> Hatred and suffering in this world.
> Were I to wish you peace this evening,
> I would wish you peace!

At the end of our read-through, the cathartic release of tension was so palpable that even the most hardheaded among us was deeply touched; the spiritual healing that swirled through the room as the choir's final chord drifted into the far reaches of the sanctuary caused forty normally rambunctious Unitarian Universalists to sit in stunned silence for over a minute.

But the story does not end there. The next day, one of the altos felt particularly uneasy at work because all of her colleagues were gathered around the television set, rooting for the American bombers over Baghdad as if they were watching a football game. Even though the corporate culture in her office strongly discouraged voicing any anti-war opinions, she sensed that one of her co-workers shared her disapproval of the Bush administration's handling of the Persian Gulf situation. But she was afraid to broach the subject directly because her supervisor had warned her to keep her opinions to herself. Over lunch she approached her co-worker indirectly, cautiously discussing some of her hobbies and interests outside work, including her church choir. Out of politeness, the co-worker asked her what pieces her choir was currently rehearsing. Imagine his surprise when she quoted the Reverend Hurto's poem in its entirety, a feat made possible because melodies have long been known to help human memory. (Children learn their ABCs most quickly when they sing them to a nursery tune.) The poem so interested the co-worker that he decided to attend the Unitarian church nearest his home the next Sunday. To make a long story short, he gained a spiritual home, and the church gained a new member.

All of the advantages that adult volunteer choirs bring to liberal churches are doubled when the choir consists of children. My first public performance occurred at age six, when as a member of Mrs. Bell's newly formed Presbyterian Cherub Choir, I sang "I'll Be a Sunbeam for Jesus" in a sunflower costume. For the first time in anyone's memory, the church was full; there is nothing quite like a children's choir to bring out the parental "captive audience." Within a year of Mrs. Bell's arrival in my small rural town, she had formed six different children's choirs and the church membership had grown from eighty to 300.

Although the hymnal and the volunteer choir (both adult and children's choirs) are the music program's most powerful agents to help facilitate church growth, many other options remain open to the enterprising UU Music Director. Well-played instrumental music, for example, is usually received well by Unitarian Universalists because its abstract nature appeals to the intellect while its emotional component enthralls the spirit. But instrumental music, unlike choral music, requires more than performers, it requires instruments!

Professional violinists, flutists, and guitarists can, of course, be expected to bring their own instruments, but not even renowned organist E. Power Biggs traveled with his own pipe organ. Some instruments *must* be provided by the church. If a new $150,000 organ lies beyond the church's means, perhaps the congregation can purchase a used one for $20,000 from a church that is being demolished. A fine grand piano represents an even better investment because it will attract outside performing organizations that will want to use the church as both a concert site and a rehearsal space. Indeed, six years after our congregation spent $13,000 on a nine-foot concert grand piano, we were able to recover all of the expenses through building rentals because we had one of the best pianos in town. More than one of our new members first stepped inside the church to attend a secular concert made possible because of that piano, but returned because of the UU pamphlets they read during the intermission. Our church is now investigating the purchase of a harpsichord because of a growing interest in hearing early music played on authentic instruments.

Fortunately, the benefits of purchasing instruments for the church are not limited to "big ticket items" like organs and pianos. Hand chimes and finger cymbals can add inestimable charm to a Christmas Eve service, while tambourines, bongo drums, and castanets can enliven the most staid hymn. Xylophones and hand bells not only provide beautiful accompaniments to anthems and hymns, they are excellent teaching tools in an era when declining tax revenues are forcing schools to eliminate music programs. Many fifth grade boys who wouldn't be caught dead singing in a choir will gladly learn to beat a drum or ring a bell. Recorders and similar "easy" instruments provide enjoyment for children of all ages and are particularly useful in forging intergenerational musical ensembles.

The potential for attracting newcomers to our churches through music is limited only by the imagination and energy of its members. Some Unitarian Universalist congregations sponsor weekly recitals or annual music festivals; others offer participatory programs for the general public (*Messiah* Sing-A longs, do-it-yourself Gilbert and Sullivan shows, Sacred Harp conventions, etc.). Many UU churches offer space to arts organizations that no other denomination in town will even consider, such as gay and lesbian choruses; others support Wiggle Worms, Suzuki, Montessori, and other alternative music programs for children. Some of our most exciting music outreach programs send teams of church members to nursing homes (in months other than December), hospitals, prisons, soup kitchens, and other places where live entertainment is in short supply.

But, in the end, it matters not whether music offered in the service of transcending love is performed by a paid professional, volunteer choristers, or children. Nor does it matter whether the intended audience consists of church members on a Sunday morning, the general public on a Saturday evening, or a group of AIDS patients on a Monday afternoon. What matters most, more than the size of the group or the perfection of the rendition, is the spirit in which the music is offered. A hymn that touches the heart or an anthem that stirs the soul will always kindle the amazing grace that inspires us all.

Evangelizing Our Children

Tony A. Larsen

Parents tell me continuously that they do not give their children any religious training, from the feeling that it is taking unfair advantage of the child. They say, "I propose to let my children grow up as far as possible unbiased." [But] if you do not bias [your children], the first one that [they] meet on the street, or in school, or among [their] companions, will begin the work of biasing, of the impression of education, for this is a continuous process. Whether you will it or not, it is something over which you have no choice. It is something that will be done either wisely and well—or unwisely and ill.

—the Reverend Minot-Judson Savage,
19th-century Unitarian minister

MOST UNITARIAN UNIVERSALISTS are come-outers. In fact, eighty-five to ninety percent of those who are UUs today were not raised as UUs. They come either from other churches or from none. In one way, this is a testament to the validity of our religion: It is so powerful and attractive, it could stay alive without its members ever having children. We would just keep pulling in people from the outside who realize what a good deal we have going here and never have to worry about making sure our kids carry on. And in fact, that's what we have been doing, in effect. It's nothing short of miraculous. We've got to be the most nonproselytizing, nonmissionary, laid-back church in America. Nationwide, we have terrible publicity. (The truth is, we don't have terrible publicity. We have practically no publicity.) Pollsters tell us that sixty percent of the US population have never heard of us.

And yet, we still survive. We must be doing something right, because people keep coming in and replenishing our membership, and we never have to recruit our children.

Now, here's the part where I'm going to sound like a heretic to some, but I'm going to say it anyway: I think we should be recruiting our children. If we are doing this well without converting our kids, think how well we could do if we did!

Oh, I know, I know. We want our kids to make their own choices. We don't want to push our beliefs on them. We don't want to shove our religion down their throats (as perhaps our parents shoved theirs down ours). We want our kids to be free.

That's nice. And I agree with it. Our children should make their own religious choices. But that doesn't mean we can't give a plug for our religion so they're more inclined to make the best choice. And while I agree that we shouldn't push our beliefs on our children, we can at least share our beliefs with them. In the intergenerational activities I have done with UU parents and kids, I have discovered that most children do not know what their parents believe about God and afterlife and Christianity. And most parents don't know what their children believe. Now, I know we don't want to force our children to believe what we do under threat of torture, but is it too much heresy to suggest that we sit down together and talk about our beliefs? That's not shoving our religion down their throats. Sharing is different from shoving.

I say: Tell your children what you believe and why. And listen to their beliefs. And tell them why you belong to a

Unitarian Universalist congregation. And—heresy of heresies—tell them you hope they will be Unitarian Universalists when they grow up, too. That's right. Of course you will love them whether they do or not, and of course they should feel free to leave or stay. But this is a good religion, and it's doing good things. It's going to need people to keep on doing good things. And nothing is wrong with telling our kids we hope they will keep up the good work.

I know this is a radical idea among some UUs. Nevertheless, I am not content with the idea of giving our children the warm feeling of a church community but no understanding of their religion. I want them to know what it is and know how to explain it when their peers ask them about it. And I want them to know how to defend their beliefs when other children come around proselytizing.

Believe me, most UU children I know would not have been a match for me when I was a kid. When I was young I went around the neighborhood spreading the fear of hell and the wrath of God; and boy, was I good at it. Sometimes I would walk around in my little priest outfit and sprinkle holy water here and there. And sometimes I would invite the other children to come to the church my dad built for me in the backyard, and I'd tell them all about the Catholic religion. If the children were Catholic but not going to church, I would remind them of the hellfire awaiting them if they should die. If they were Protestant, I'd tell them that being Protestant didn't automatically keep them out of heaven, but it sure made it difficult to get there. I was the kind of child that most UU parents try to protect their children from! (You ought to be glad I wasn't born 35 years later in your community, because your kids would have been no match for me.)

That is why I say we should teach our children how to defend their beliefs. If you don't prepare your kids in religion, there may be a little Tony Larsen in your neighborhood who will.

One of the liberal fallacies today is: "If I don't put any restrictive religion in my child's mind, he or she will grow up free." That's as illogical as saying, "If I don't teach my child about sex, he or she won't ever try anything." We don't get a choice about whether our kids learn about sex or religion. Our only choice is who they hear about it from first.

I like what the Romantic poet Samuel Taylor Coleridge once said to a visitor. The visitor told Coleridge that he believed children should not be given any religious instruction. Then, when they grew up, said the man, they would be free to choose their own faith, without bias.

Coleridge didn't argue with the man, but he did decide to show him his backyard, which was overgrown with weeds. He told the man, "I'd like to show you my garden," but when the man saw it, he exclaimed, "Do you call this a garden? There is nothing but weeds here!" Coleridge replied, "I did not wish to infringe upon the liberty of the garden in any way. I was just giving the garden a chance to express itself and to choose its own production."

Children will learn about religion whether we teach them about it or not. But if we want them to have healthy beliefs, we must "infringe upon their liberty" by cultivating a decent garden.

So, to continue with my heresy, I think we need to do some curriculum changing in some of our Sunday schools around the country. I think we need less science, less social studies, less anthropology, and less psychology. Not that these aren't good, but we only have our kids in Sunday school about 40 hours a year—and that's only if they attend regularly, which many of them do not. Besides, these subjects are often covered in public school. In the little time we have them, I think we should teach them the following instead:

1. *How to pronounce our name*. "What church do you go to?" "Uh, Una —, Una — something like that." My gosh, that ought to be a minimum requirement.

I am reminded of the story someone told me about her daughter. It seems they had moved to a new neighborhood and her daughter was meeting some of the other children on the block. One of them asked her, "What religion are you?" Now, this little girl had been attending the nursery at the Unitarian Universalist Church, but her mother wasn't sure she remembered the name. So she waited to hear what her daughter would say. The kids kept asking her, "What religion are you?" And finally the daughter said, "Well, I'm not sure. But I think we're League of Women Voters."

2. *We should teach our children to answer to the question: What do Unitarian Universalists believe*? In a sense, this question is not the right question to ask a UU because our religion is more a way of life, a process, rather than a creed or set of dogmas. Inasmuch as most people haven't even heard of us, however, we can't expect them to ask the right kind of question of us. They are going to ask what would be appropriate to ask most other religions: What do you believe? And we should have an answer to that question. We should teach our children an answer to that question so they don't say, "Oh, we believe whatever we want to" or "We believe in freedom of belief" (which doesn't say a whole lot) or "Gee, I don't know." Because you don't get to believe just anything you want to in Unitarian Universalism. Belief in the KKK or the Nazis or bigotry—and a host of other things—are not tolerated here. So people don't get to believe just anything they want to here, and we also stand for much more than freedom of belief, as important as that is.

At our church we teach our children the following answer to the question, which you may or may not wish to use: We believe in (1) loving your neighbor as yourself, which includes trying not to steal, lie, kill, or hurt people in any other way; (2) making the world a better place, which includes working for justice, peace, and freedom for all people; and (3) searching for the truth with an open mind.

Fairly simple. Someone could improve on it, I'm sure. But in the meantime it's a fairly workable definition, and it gives our children an answer to the most frequently asked question about our church.

Evangelizing Our Children

When our eighth graders prepare for their Affirmation ceremony, they are required to learn the seven principles of the Unitarian Universalist Association. This too is a good answer to the question, "What do UUs believe?"

3. *We should teach our children how to express—and argue for—their beliefs*, as soon as they are old enough to have some. That means that as adults we should share our own beliefs and our reasons for holding them. It also means we should encourage our children to decide what they believe and teach them how to explain it to others. Some of the things they believe will be different from yours—maybe you believe in heaven when you die, and they believe in reincarnation; maybe you believe God is a force or an idea, and they believe in a supreme being. But many of your beliefs will be the same, because they are part of our UU heritage. These beliefs we should help our children to learn to express and defend by giving them practice through role-playing or some other method. For example:

> *Question:* What can you say if someone asks you if you believe in Christ as your Savior?
> *Answer:* I can say, "I believe that Jesus lived and taught things that are valuable for living, but I also believe that many others have too, so the world has many saviors and I revere all who have tried to help their fellow man and woman."
>
> *Question:* What can you say if someone tells you that people who don't accept Christ will go to hell?
> *Answer:* "You have a right to your belief, but it doesn't make sense to me. I can't believe in a God who would do such an unchristian thing."

The children from other religions learn their church's pet doctrines and favorite passages; is it really fair to our kids not to let them know what to expect or how to express and defend their faith?

4. *I believe we should teach our children more Unitarian and Universalist history.* Tell our kids about some of their forebears who tried to make this a better world. Then at least when someone says, "Unitarian Universalist? Never heard of it," they can answer, "Well, have you heard of Thomas Jefferson or Susan B. Anthony or Ralph Waldo Emerson?" Of course, more important than giving them a reply to make is the sense of tradition and identity that learning our history will give them.

5. *We should teach the Bible* for three reasons: (a) because some good lessons and words of wisdom and inspiring thought are in it, (b) because knowing more about the Bible from a historical perspective will enable our children to defend their beliefs better (since, let's face it, most of the other side will be Bible believers), and (c) because this is a Judeo-Christian culture and anyone who doesn't know anything about the Bible is culturally illiterate. Someone told me about a friend of hers who had had no religious training, and when a reference was made in one of her college classes to David and Goliath, she had no idea what they were talking about. That's not fair to our children. They deserve to know the myths and symbols and stories that make up our culture, and the Bible is a part of that.

I once told the following to a group of high-school UUs:

> There was one Universalist who said to another one, "I'll bet you can't say the Lord's Prayer."
>
> And the second one said, "I'll bet you five bucks I can."
>
> "OK," said the first, "you're on."
>
> So the second one recited: "Now I lay me down to sleep, I pray the Lord my soul to keep. If I should die before I wake, I pray the Lord my soul to take."
>
> And the first Unitarian looked at the second one and said, "All right, you win."

What bothered me when I told this joke to the high-schoolers is that nobody got it! None of them knew the Lord's Prayer either. I think we owe them more than that. And teaching the Bible from a historical perspective would go a long way toward improving their cultural literacy.

6. *We should teach our children more about world religions*. I put this under the Bible in importance only because our kids don't actually need to know this in order to defend their beliefs or understand our culture. But knowing about the religions of the world can be very helpful for our children, because it not only encourages tolerance of other cultures and a feeling of being a world citizen, but it helps them see Christianity and the Bible in perspective. When other kids tell them Jesus was born of a virgin, for example, they can answer, "That's what lots of religions say about their founders. Buddha was born of a virgin too. So was Lao-Tse, the founder of Taoism, and How-Tsieh, the founder of China, and Zoroaster, the founder of Zoroastrianism." When other children talk about a judgment day, our kids could explain to them that that idea came from the Zoroastrians, centuries before Christ—as did heaven and hell and angels and devils. They could also explain how the Jews picked it up from the Zoroastrians, the Christians picked it up from the Jews, and the Muslims picked it up from both.

When someone tells them that Jesus is the messiah or savior, our children will understand the Zoroastrians believed there would be a savior too and so did the Jews, and they would understand why Jews today do not feel Jesus fit the prophecies of the messiah. They would understand that not only the Zoroastrians and Jews and Christians taught the coming of a messiah, but the Shiite Muslims, Hindus, and certain Buddhist sects as well.

When other children say that Jesus is God, our children would understand why Jews and Muslims consider that idolatry. But they would also see why the fourth-century Christian bishops voted to make Jesus God, because they would understand humanity's need to do that with its heroes. They would know that many Buddhists later made Buddha a god (even though he was probably an agnostic), and that Hinduism has its own incarnations of God, for Vishnu is said to have come down to earth in human form through Ram and Krishna and many other saviors.

And when confronted with the doctrine of the trinity and other beliefs about God, our children would see that some religions in the world believe in one God, some believe in many Gods, some believe in no God, and some (like Hinduism and Christianity) are combinations of several of the above. They would learn that monotheism and polytheism and atheism all have something to teach us.

Other churches don't usually explain all these things to their children. They are usually only interested in teaching Christianity and usually just their version of it. Some of them don't want their kids to know too much about the religions of the world. As a result, most people don't learn about any of this until they take a world religions class in college, if then. If we taught these things to our children, they could go from being theological illiterates to being religious experts. Instead of not knowing what the other kids are even talking about, UU kids would know that and more. Unitarian Universalist churches are in a unique position to offer a broader, more in-depth religious education to our children. We don't have anything standing in our way. There are no creeds or dogmas that we have to worry about sidestepping. There are no fundamentalists in our congregations to insist that the Bible be taught as the literal word of God. We could do it. We could change our youth from being more ignorant than their peers in religious matters to being theologically better informed than the average.

7. We should teach our children ethics. The reason I've put ethics in at number seven instead of higher, is because I presume our children are getting moral training at home. Actually, I believe this is more important than any other aspect of religious up bringing. If they are not getting it at home, then it should take top priority in Sunday school.

Evangelizing Our Children

These are the areas I'd concentrate on if I were in charge of redesigning church school curricula. The psychology, the social studies, the science, the anthropology—these are all fine too, but we have our children in Sunday school only forty hours a year. Let's use that time to prepare them for the religious world they are living in and teach them the things they are not going to learn accurately anywhere else. They will learn some of those other subjects in public school, but they won't learn about religion there, at least not in an objective way.

It might also be a good idea if we let them know that we would like for them to continue in the church of their fathers and mothers. I know we probably would survive without them, for a while at least, but wouldn't it be nice to have them standing alongside us and carrying on the torch—and then passing it in turn to their children and their grandchildren?

If we want that to happen, we need to give them a feeling of UU identity and a sense of belonging to Unitarian Universalism. We can't simply say, "I hope the UU Church will meet your needs when you're an adult." Who ever heard of joining a church only because it meets your needs? That is part of it, of course, but a UU church also exists to serve outside itself. It exists to help save the world from war and bigotry and hatred and ignorance.

After all, if we were just worried about ourselves, our congregations would become rather boring places. We would do better in a rap group or a counseling session. So rather than telling our children, "I hope the UU church will meet your needs," I think we should be saying, "I hope you will stick with the UU church and help it meet the needs of the wider human community—whether it meets your personal needs or not. Because the needs of the wider community are what it is primarily there to serve. And it can't do that without people like you."

If we said that, maybe our children would know we really believe Unitarian Universalism is important. I know they don't absolutely need the UU church. And I know you don't absolutely need the UU church. But that's not the point. The point is that the world needs the UU church. The world needs voices of reason, and it needs voices of compassion. And those are the two main things Unitarianism and Universalism have stood for, these past 400 years.

> Honi ha-Ma'aggel once saw on his travels an old man planting a carob tree. He asked him when he thought the tree would bear fruit.
>
> "Oh, after about seventy years," was the reply.
>
> "Do you really expect to live seventy years and eat the fruit of your labor?" asked ha-Ma'aggel.
>
> "Well," said the old man, "I didn't find the world desolate when I entered it. And since my forebears planted for me before I was born, so do I plant for those who will come after me."
>
> —from the Gemarra (Jewish)

Inclusive Evangelism

Robert W. Karnan

I AM TOLD BY Charles Gaines, Director of the UUA Department of Extension, that the congregation I serve as Senior Minister has been the fastest growing UU congregation for the past five years. I have no way to prove it other than to show the scars on my body and my soul. He also has said that South Church in Portsmouth, New Hampshire, is one of the very few UU societies for some decades to grow from small through middle to large size. Many of us are aware of a large number of wonderful congregations and fine ministries that are beacons of inspiration and example. I want to share with you a short outline of the recent history of South Church in Portsmouth, New Hampshire, and then suggest why all our Unitarian Universalist congregations matter.

Much of the growth in South Church has occurred during a period in which our local economy was devastated and the population of the city dropped by twenty percent in three years. Portsmouth is now at just over 20,000 residents. We have lost an air force base and a vast number of small businesses. There have been too many layoffs and reductions in force. We have not been able to afford UUA pamphlets and do not have them

Inclusive Evangelism

to explain to visitors who we are and what our movement is about. The church has no parking lot. It is located in the downtown area and is surrounded within a few blocks by six other churches and a synagogue. It is an old building (1824) that is cold and drafty in the winter and hot and stuffy in the summer. The average age of our membership is just below thirty-seven but includes people of all ages. It is not a baby boomer facility by any measure—there are no designer landscapes, interior decorating, or modern facilities (of the three bathrooms in the building only one has hot water). It is an unmistakably historic building of Greek Revival vintage with the Lord's Prayer and "Love Thy Neighbor As Thyself" biblical verses prominently guilded on the front walls of the sanctuary. These words have been with the congregation in their various buildings as their "motto" since its founding in 1627.

In 1977 the congregation determined to change itself from being only an old historic church to a more inclusive and dynamic religious society. They called a young and able minister who began that process. Hard changes had to be faced about worship and religious education and the values and culture of the congregation. There was some struggle and some heartache, but the process of a new vision began and it continued even after that minister left to go elsewhere.

When I was called, the members thought they numbered about 266. Actually, the official list was about 124. After I visited and talked around for several months, I found that the real active and participating membership was 55. There were 33 pledges totaling an amount of about $19,000. We collected a little under $13,000 in pledges that year. The legal membership is today just over 740, and there are about another 300 persons active in the life of the congregation.

What we learned in this decade of growth and change could fill several books. What I want to share is a short summary. We found that there is a strong, almost universal culture about church life that envisions for the most part small congregations and a professional religious leadership that ministers to that culture. It includes dependence on powerful central lay figures who dominate the life of the congregation and carry its culture and history and protect it from danger and changes. Ministers are encouraged to pastor and relate well, but preaching and worship are not the highest priority and are not rewarded as completely as is pastoring conscientiously.

We found that in order to create a more inclusive and diverse future, the minister had to turn away from a focus on the inner life of the congregation and its existing members and instead had to look outward to the community and possible new members. We found that the service of worship had to be of high quality each week. The preaching had to be good, the music fine, and the religious education for children fully functional and responsive to parent concerns. We found that if we did these things we attracted and held a new and diverse membership and we grew consistently weekly, monthly, and yearly. This has been the case for a decade and more.

We found that the professional ministry had to focus on the larger community and the social and moral issues there and also on newcomers and their concerns and on future envisioning. We found that wholly new structures of inner congregational relationship and pastoral caring and ministry had to be created. A concept of lay ministries evolved along with a visitation committee, and a pastoral component was conceived for almost every program or activity. It was an empowerment of the laity to minister, while at the same time an empowerment of the professional religious leadership. The two, we found, work hand in hand and must work hand in hand. The congregation had to learn all over again what democracy is about, for in an inclusive setting the ability to coordinate and cooperate is central, and the power centers must be diffused to many different facets and corners of the organization.

Inclusive congregational membership means intentionally opening the doors and pews with a genuine welcome to all who come in goodwill. It means a natural concomitant fear among the existing members about the many unknown people who begin to sit next to and join in worship with those who have been there for a long time. We found that this is the frontier for confrontation with racism, class phobia, ageism, genderism, homophobia, and all the other prejudices that we hold mostly privately just under the surface of our daily lives. Those who felt the invitation to come and to join came in great variety. What is certain is that they dramatically opened the spiritual life of the congregation and brought with them language, concerns, questions, doubts, and focused interests that had not been much expressed previously.

An inclusive opening brings discomfort. The discomfort exists for those who are already members, and it exists for the newcomer too. The growth of South Church must actually be measured by the ability of each of the participants to generously open themselves to others who are quite different, and in the deepening of relationship that has consequently become the center of the congregation's religious life. We have found one another in our great variety, and thus we have found ourselves. It has meant reformation in language, ritual, form, process, and confrontation with assumptions of privilege and prerogative. The new and palpable affirmations are about overcoming sexism or homophobia or racism in our lives as we live them, and not only in the lives of Susan B. Anthony or votes of legislatures or the passage of a Martin Luther King Day for New Hampshire.

The journey has meant that we speak more honestly and listen carefully. It has meant a growth of the heart and the spirit of love to encompass more than the congregation has previously been willing to see and to know. It has meant becoming a close friend to someone who ten years ago might have been avoided because of their identity or looks or presumed status. We have begun to remake our world, beginning with ourselves, and the transformation has been as liberating as it has been demanding. Honest and open being together has meant a powerful unifying resolve to see a healthier and safer world, and it has brought us a sense of inner peace. For we know through experience that we can move in a common spirit to heal our own brokenness and address the sufferings of our community.

We are human, and we have made mistakes in this quest for deepening and opening. To learn is to err time and again, but we seek to do so openly and in the community of many who are searching as well to create a context of truthfulness and spiritual vulnerability that is ferociously alive and generative and transforming. Come into such a place, and it is both a relief and a challenge. It is as radically Unitarian Universalist as we can make it, and it is a heavenly mixture of political, spiritual, theological, and social transformation. The story of South Church is carried mostly by word of mouth, although in recent years the church has been featured in the local newspapers and acknowledged for its uniqueness and vitality as well in the Sunday magazine of the *Boston Globe*.

When we reached midsize, the plans for our future began to gel. We renovated our building and began to invite into our frantic midst more support and professional staff. We purchased a new education building (actually, an old apartment house next door) and changed our organizational and governance structure and created all the councils and committees and programs that typify a large congregation. And we have grown into that configuration. It became necessary to create a vast array of small group settings and coordinate them well so that we could be with one another in close, friendly ways. The church now has two services on Sunday and a weekly vespers. The adult learning program is large and diverse. We struggle with keeping up with our expansion, we struggle with raising enough money, and we struggle with no parking and with an old building that is in use constantly and requires continual upkeep.

But this is not how we view ourselves as a Unitarian Universalist congregation. Rather, we see ourselves as a place of religion and of spiritual journey and social conscience and doing what is just and right. We know we are thoroughly inclusive and as diverse as our community. We are atheists and theists, pagans and trinitarians, the confused and the certain. We are stimulated by our sharing, and we have yet to have a fight about religion or theology. We are able to approach most of what we do with a spirit of healing and honesty and humility.

One of our recent members is a former Associate Minister of the Crystal Cathedral in California. He still thinks in and uses the language of enthusiastic religion. He used the word "mission" to describe the goals of our congregation and was gently rebuked by one of our older members who told him, "We UUs don't use that word."

"Of course we do," he replied with a laugh, "I'm a UU and I use it, and it would probably be a good idea if more of us did."

He went on to observe that our nation is in the midst of a dramatic shift in religious consciousness and that one of the more significant changes is that we are a lot smarter today, probably because of so many broken promises churches make so regularly, to wit that they are the only ones who serve God's love. We now demand to see the genuine quality of a church before we join it. In times past the denomination was important or perhaps the status of the congregation in the community. Today it is the honesty of the experience in the congregation and the real justice it serves, the love it actually sustains, and the vision it holds for itself. It has a mission for its members, for the community, and for the world. It is a church alive!

Such a church now is almost certainly inclusive. It is peopled by those of genuine goodwill and true allegiance, who serve not a conventional social identity but a living expectation and commitment to depth of relationship and effective social transformation. The test of membership is not social standing or education or race or gender or sexual identity or age or any other shallow criterion. It is genuine willingness to subject oneself to the turmoil and the balm of honest engagement with all who come in goodwill and who do not violate that trust with deceit, abusive behavior, or insincere participation.

Something more, however, should be said. Churches do little that is tangible or obviously measurable. There is no clear bottom line that all might agree on. Some cite attendance as a sort of measure, others the numbers of people "saved" for

Jesus. In Unitarian Universalist circles, we are likely to hear about the great numbers at the Christmas Eve service or who came out for a special dinner. A few measure the numbers of dollars they have accrued, and a few more look to their buildings and possessions. I have heard a couple of churches and denominations point to the number of employees with special pride. Probably the most usual bottom line that measures the value of a church is its size. Recently, one church put in its newsletter that it valued itself highly because of the number of food baskets they had managed to give away last Christmas. Churches and synagogues that grow often report that they feel good about themselves, and those that are not growing report not feeling so good.

These are all fairly ordinary thoughts about churches, and probably many of us have held them from time to time. But I want to say clearly that hardly a soul seeks out and joins a congregation because it gives away food baskets or because it has a big net worth or owns a great building or has thousands of people in attendance. We do not gather with the thought in mind to balance a budget and make a treasurer happy and an accountant content. We do not come to worship or to meet or in one another's homes time and again to fix the roof leaks and make sure that the old furnace continues to huff and puff for still one more season. No one has yet told me that the true reason they go to services or belong to a congregation is to guarantee a justly earned retirement for the minister in which she/he will, with full satisfaction, gum animal crackers, guzzle Postum, and cackle about the "good old days."

Ministers are sometimes asked what they do. What is being asked normally is what busywork did we occupy ourselves with: office conferences, meetings attended, sermons written, funerals conducted. What is not being asked is the bottom line to which we hold ourselves: the all too satisfied who were invited to rethink their lives, those who are now suffering given not only solace but permission to take the power available to them to heal and to seek righteousness where it has been denied, the deepened relationships that mean that our deaths are not a raw aching tragedy but simply a heartfelt and loving grief.

Our churches and fellowships matter because they are places of the spirit, temples of forgiveness, synagogues of compassion, mosques of meaning in powerful and enduring friendship, congregations of courage and of love set free to transform and to face the times of our lives with an honesty that casts out fear and invites peace.

Churches and ministry are about human liberation. Liberation from fear and loathing and ugly self-destruction. Liberation from excess pleasures and undue comforts that prevent us from feeling fully the unrighteousness that is all around us; it is giving the depth of our hearts to those with whom we would very much want to share them. The task is to set free forces of love and justice that may scare as much as they might delight. If we look to the quest for racial justice in this nation and more particularly at the civil rights successes of the 1950s and 1960s, we find that the churches were at the foundation. When the Reverend Martin Luther King, Jr., set off to confront this nation with love and with nonviolence in order to bring justice to all, he carried in his heart not only that love but a fear too for what he might set loose. The nonviolent civil rights era was rife with blood and tears, violence and death. And yet, in spite and because of it, this nation created for itself a deeper understanding that endures even as fairness and justice remain unfulfilled.

The Board Chair of South Church shared a comment recently that bears repeating. We were talking about the things a church does that are identified as social justice activities. He mentioned how in his many years as a UU most churches have thought that some committee or another did something special for the needy, or held a forum discussion, or organized a demonstration against an injustice—and thought that it worked for social justice. But, he noted, the whole identity of a good church is that it speaks and acts for the transformation of our lives at all levels simultaneously: spiritual, emotional, intellectual, and moral. The church, he said, is in its entirety a social action organization. The task of the church is to make over our lives as they need it and our society as it requires it.

We recently asked the members of our Board to share at the beginning of a recent meeting what they experience as the worth of their church to them. In aggregate this is what they said:

South Church inspires me to live more honestly, more fully, more completely. It allows me to reach out to others. As a confirmed non-churchgoer for twenty-five years, I was amazed to see how this church has enriched my life. Through the fellowship, music, the education, and the sharing of much laughter and many tears, it has lifted my soul and taught my family and me new meanings of human kinship.

Here I can be my most authentic self, the "real" me without fear of judgment or criticism, at least not without a large dollop of loving care, understanding, and respect. Here I can express and discuss my spiritual concerns, my greatest longings as a human being. Here I can count on others in times of great need and great joy; both live here always, and I can come back to them whenever I choose. I had my wedding here along with the deepest sadness at my father's death. Here my greatest questions live, along with the answers.

South Church has a story, and we live together as a community. What drives us forward is that story: It is big enough to be inclusive of everybody; it is made of companionship and love, social concerns and hospitality, spirituality and mystery. It touches me deep inside and gives me strength.

It is a happy sense of belonging to a multi-aged group where I can partake alone and with others. It is a religious community celebrating our differences while seeking the common humanity that unites us across race, gender, and culture.

Inclusive Evangelism

One of our members in her recent application essay to a graduate degree program wrote a compelling, grateful letter of spiritual growth that came from her Unitarian Universalist participation.

> Now, when I look back at the [tender] age of thirty in an attempt to gain perspective, I see clearly that my search for individual meaning and the desire to make sense of my life all coalesce around the experience of spiritual healing that began in South Church in Portsmouth, New Hampshire. When I came to South Church, I was hungry for spiritual satisfaction, but not filled by my experimentation with several different Protestant denominations and the Roman Catholicism of my childhood. Until then I was ashamed to be a lesbian and unable to hold my head high with quiet pride instead of with bitter defiance. Within my church I have become a whole person. In the open-hearted, open-minded congregation on State Street in Portsmouth, I have realized that not only could I allow myself to be accepted by a diverse community, but that I too could accept a diverse community.

Our churches and fellowships exist to speak for something and to something a great deal more compelling and significant and powerful than size or buildings or money. They exist, and have for these long years, to bring us together in kindness and honesty and to give us the gift of our deep and good friendships. They also invite us, if we need the invitation, to listen to the cries of injustice and of pain and to do something curative about them. They invite us to share our woes, our tears, our laughter, and our joy. They ask us to share our lost moments and our insanity as well as our found ones and our sanity. For each of us has all of these at some time or another. They request our honest presence so that we may share the goodness that honesty brings. It is not Truth that they seek, but the truths of the mind and heart as we seek and find and lose and find them anew together.

Our church and fellowship buildings and the moments we share within and outside of them point to a sometimes wild and raging visionary courage in the face of all that would demean and destroy and pervert and estrange what is in our hearts. There is no more critical task for our lives than the courage to love and to be there honestly and fully for one another. Deep and good friendship and all the trust and serenity that come with it are transformative. Deep friendship makes a healthy life possible, even likely. It makes for peace and for strength in facing the hardest issues. Doing what we can for what is right, just, and fair here where we live is the most powerful social justice force on earth.

Our task as a religious society is not to idolize and love God, it is to love one another in just relationship so that we make the love of God a reality and not a desperate dream or a painful despair. The love of God that is in the yearning of our hearts is that which we deserve, that is justified by the vision we hold and the love we give away and the courage we hold fiercely within. It is in our ability to be a human community of peace and to do what is good and right.

The quality of the love and goodness we expose from our sometimes reluctant hearts will change the world. Our task is not to make more UUs or to make bigger congregations or to raise great gobs of money. It is to heal and to inspire, to open and to remake, and thus change what is sorry to what is a joy. It is why we gather in the spirit of love and justice. It is why I give my life in service to what can only be described as invisible and intangible but which is also the most powerful force of all: our all too human, sometimes faltering, sometimes complete, sometimes painful and sad, sometimes serene and laughing love— that speaks, if anything at all does, with the voice of God.

May our vision so soar that no budget is possible to contain it, may our love of justice be so genuine that no community can thwart its cleansing healing goodness, may our courage overcome all fear and set the spirit free.

Ideas for Congregational Growth

Dangerous Myths

William Burnside Miller

THERE I SAT attending service the Sunday after Christmas with my son-in-law, a devout Roman Catholic. My wife and I had flown north on the twenty-fifth to celebrate the holidays with our children and grandchildren. When New Year's Sunday arrived, I decided to attend service at the local outpost of free religion. Our theologically staunch, though nonmember, Unitarian Universalist daughter decided to join me with her husband.

It was a delight to enter the attractive meeting house. When we were greeted I did not identify myself as a minister. Sometimes it is nice to be a civilian. On glancing at the order of service, I discovered that the resident minister was not to be the speaker of the morning. I was somewhat disappointed, but then reminded myself that anyone attending service that day at my home society would also be hearing someone other than the settled cleric.

The Sunday after Christmas was apparently something of a tradition for this congregation. It turned out to be a lay-led celebration consisting of a collection of bits and pieces played, sung, and spoken by members and friends. Some of the musical contributions were good. Regrettably, most of the prose and poetry selections were not. They ranged from the maudlin to the malignant and were presented with a grinding solemnity.

After nearly an hour of intense, personal sharing with nary a mention of any recognizable theological construct, the service leader made his way to the center of the pulpit platform. He took from his pocket a pair of lensless spectacles to which was attached a plastic pig's snout and placed them on his nose. He then proceeded to recite a piece that extolled the joys of using outdoor toilet facilities.

When the closing words were finally uttered I raced for the door. My overwhelming response was one of embarrassment. On the basis of this worship experience, what could my son-in-law possibly conclude about Unitarian Universalism?

Many of the things that did or did not occur in that service eloquently illustrate major weaknesses in our tradition. Although I believe that there is much that is positive in contemporary Unitarian Universalism, there is also much that demands careful examination.

Congregational growth is of deep concern to all of us committed to the future of our free faith. We have found something of great spiritual value, and we wish to share it with others. Traditionally the best way of accomplishing this has been through institutional growth. In a sense, if we do not grow, we are passing a terrible judgment on ourselves and the choices we have made. If our faith is truly wonderful, then this should be more widely recognized.

It is my belief that our hitherto lackluster growth record has been primarily the result of a dangerous institutional mythology. Perhaps the most dangerous of all myths is the belief that we want to grow. From personal observation I can attest that growth is the farthest thing from the minds of some liberal religionists. Many of our societies operate as private clubs open to members only. After all, if you have discovered "Truth," "Beauty," and "Right" and know that only a small elite can possibly attain that goal, then surely you do not want to be sullied by the intellectually, spiritually, or culturally unwashed.

We smugly congratulate ourselves on our rejection of proselytizing, grandly affirming a gracious tolerance of differing points of
view. We then sit content with our small numbers, knowing that
our way can only appeal to people who are truly superior, which
is to say people just like us. After all, if small is beautiful, then
tiny must be terrific.

Pursuing this goal of quality, purity, and tolerance our elite
can become more elite. Indeed, we may become so elite that we
are too good to live. It has long been my feeling that Unitarian
Universalists harbor a powerful institutional death wish. Whether this is the result of conscious thought or an unconscious
rejection of strategies requiring change makes no difference. The
end remains the same. It is failure.

Let us explode the growth myth once and for all. Let us
recognize that there are many UU societies that do not wish to
grow. This does not mean that members of such congregations are
traitors to the cause. It simply means they are choosing a different
way to live out their faith. Indeed, their way has been the norm
for decades. Ministries of maintenance are enthusiastically embraced by many of our churches.

Too many ministers and their congregations have come into
conflict because of a fundamental misunderstanding regarding
growth. If a congregation wants to grow and its minister does not,
growth will not occur. If a minister wants a congregation to grow
and its members do not, growth will not occur. Then too, there are
those ministers and congregations stoutly maintaining their
desire to grow while making certain that such a result could never
pertain. Growth can only occur when a mystical congruence of
true desire is manifested by both minister and members. That
manifestation alone will not guarantee growth, but it is a necessary precondition of it.

Another dangerous myth is the belief that Unitarian Universalists are absolutely unique. How often have I heard it said that
we are different from other religious groups and therefore should
never look to others for counsel or guidance. This is tantamount
to claiming infallibility. If our history since denominational

merger teaches us nothing else, it teaches us that we are frightfully fallible.

The only way I know of avoiding the repetition of past mistakes is by studying those errors and then inquiring of others how best to proceed based on their experience and understanding. If we blindly continue to assert our uniqueness, not only as Unitarian Universalists but also (worse yet) as individual congregations, we cut ourselves off from legitimate sources of inspiration for vitality and growth. I believe we have much to learn from others and that we cannot continue to indulge our affection for rugged individualism by ignoring those more institutionally successful than ourselves.

A third myth undermining our faith is the notion that we really do embody excellence in our congregations. We enjoy congratulating ourselves on our economic successes, our intellectual attainments, and our social triumphs. We are fond of reassuring ourselves of how remarkably capable we are. The problem is that because we are so convinced of our mutual superiority, it is difficult to be even the tiniest bit judgmental. How else can one possibly account for the ongoing mediocrity of services tolerated and, yes, even celebrated by many of our societies? This mediocrity may encourage near universal participation, but it does not encourage growth. Quality is an essential element in worship as it should be in all aspects of our lives.

A fourth troubling myth is the idea that informality and spontaneity are terminal values. Given our traditionally sunny view of human nature, maybe it is inevitable that we should believe that good will prevail even without thoughtful intentionality. Perhaps we have to believe that the spontaneous is always more true and sincere, whether or not life experience has vindicated this point of view.

Planning is essential, especially in the realm of worship. Wrestling with transcendent issues requires rigorous and disciplined forethought. As for informality, I believe it has its place, but that place is not in the formal worship of a community that desires greater growth and increased credibility.

For too long we have not taken ourselves seriously. We have offered a haven for those on their way out of institutionalized religion. We have demanded little and received little. Too many of us have actually espoused the notion that one can believe anything and still be a Unitarian Universalist. We have resisted the strictures imposed by form and structure and embraced a laissez-faire spirituality that has commanded the respect of nearly no one.

A fifth myth is rooted in our collective self-image. It appalls me to observe that it is the orthodox and the fundamentalists who have mastered the technologies of computers, VCRs, and broadcast media, while many of our congregations have offices that are truly Dickensian, the purveyors of yesterday's theology. We continue to rely on the print media to communicate with the world when the rest of the world has moved onto the information super highway.

A sixth unfortunate myth relates to the devotion that "real" Unitarian Universalists are supposed to have to their faith. This devotion is presumed to be so great that practical impediments to attending service are dismissed as irrelevant: Why bother advertising in the paper or yellow pages—a real Unitarian Universalist will find the way. Why build in a visible location with easy access—a real Unitarian Universalist will know where to go. Why make your congregation's home attractive and well kept—a real Unitarian Universalist disdains such pedestrian considerations. In too many communities we have built new buildings that are impossible to find without the aid of a scout. To add insult to injury we then proceed to provide inadequate parking, uncomfortable seating, and sloppy maintenance. The result of all this is to require a real test of faith on the part of any prospective member.

Our forebears who founded our historic first parishes knew the importance of location. They also knew that their houses of worship would be a lasting testimony to their faith. They wanted the meaning of their religion to be reflected in the beauty of the best architecture and finest artisanship. They knew that true devotion needed to be expressed in such a way that the proclaimed good news would be favorably heard. I submit that we can afford to do no less in our generation.

Myth number seven is centered in the unfortunate misperception that anything new or different is necessarily better. Although it is true that our understanding of religion has evolved through the centuries, it is not always true that the theology of one generation is better than the one it replaced.

Much of our sense of institutional pride comes from the belief that we occupy a "cutting edge" position in American religious thought. There is evidence that this may have been the case during parts of the nineteenth century. As for this century, I will leave it to history to determine whether or not our blade has remained sharp and well positioned.

If we are forever embracing the new and different just because they are new and different, we run the risk of becoming spiritual faddists. If we wish to describe ourselves as seekers of the truth, we beware of being merely dabbling dilettantes. We must avoid the temptation to flit from one idea to another without fully appreciating or understanding any spe-cific insight.

I suggest as well that it is not possible or even desirable to maintain the same "cutting edge" position perennially. Our role is not what it was 100 years ago and to believe that it could be again is to indulge in fantasy. Whatever it is that we become, it will be different from what we are or have been.

An eighth myth that enjoys great currency among us is the thought that all authority is evil. We educate our children and young people to be forever skeptical of figures who wield influence and power. We tend to believe that obedience and loyalty are flaws rather than virtues. It is no wonder then that we find it so difficult to build organizational structures to serve our institutional needs. Without discernible lines of authority and accountability, we founder. Mistakenly believing that we are "affirming the worth and dignity of every person," we may instead create a social chaos serving no good religious end.

It was in 1953 that the president of the American Unitarian Association, Frederick May Eliot, suggested religious liberals would have to remake themselves to realize their potential. He wrote: "They will have to make up their minds to throw aside their traditional distrust of all organization, which is in part the product of sad experience but also—and in much larger part—a kind of spiritual poverty that has no justification in fact."

Authority can be bad, but it can also be good. To dismiss authority out of hand is to preclude the growth of any social unit beyond a minuscule size.

The ninth and final myth has to do with how we relate to one another. This myth may be the most troubling of all because it has to do with how we actually live our faith. Our stated ideals regarding human behavior are lofty indeed. They encompass insights from the great religious traditions of the world, and they challenge us to become ever more humane. At least in theory, we are the kindest and nicest of people. The problem is that our actions speak so much more accurately and eloquently than our words. Often under the guise of honesty, integrity, or authenticity we feel commissioned to say and do the most ungracious things. There is no other way I can account for what I have witnessed in many of our congregations. This may be the reason why our books do not reflect the thousands of people who identified themselves as Unitarian Universalists in a recent survey, but are not recorded as members of any congregation.

For the past twenty-one years I have practiced the Unitarian Universalist ministry. During that period it has been my pleasure to be a part of congregational growth in every church I have served. For the past ten years I have been minister of the Unitarian Universalist Church in Fort Myers, Florida. During that period the membership has grown from approximately 150 to 400. The budget has nearly quadrupled, and a trio of buildings has been constructed on a new site. Our capital investment thus far has been roughly $1.3 million. We still have additional church school space to construct as well as a hall of worship to build.

If my experience in Fort Myers has taught me nothing else, it has taught me that ministry is partnership. It has also taught me that our fondest dreams can be realized if they are shared.

Dangerous Myths

Even as I believe that we are often our own worst enemies, I also believe that we are often prevented from achieving institutional success because of some of the myths I have described. I believe that revealing these myths for what they are is essential.

Much of the success of our Fort Myers society has to do with the fact that both the members of the congregation and I desired growth. We honestly shared a common goal and then set about to realize it with great intentionality. One of our members did not want growth. From the beginning of my ministry he made it clear that he liked the church as it was. The larger we grew the more unhappy he became. He said again and again that when the congregation moved to its new home he would resign. This man kept his word. I will always honor him for his forthrightness, but I am most grateful his views and actions constituted a minority of one.

In our growth process we have constantly reached out for counsel and advice. We have listened to gurus of growth both from the UUA as well as from other less doctrinally pure sources. We have looked with respect, admiration, and sometimes even envy at what other congregations have wrought.

As we have grown in numbers we have tried to offer more programs, always keeping a close eye on the quality of what we offered. A two-service Sunday morning format has been adopted to meet the needs of our expanding congregation during the Florida high season. Wednesday evening programming, including various opportunities for socialization, lay-led worship, and discussion has been enthusiastically received.

Much of what has been accomplished has been the result of careful planning. Long- and short-term goals have been identified, and strategies for implementation defined. Administratively we have streamlined our procedures by obtaining and using current technologies. This does not mean that we are state of the art, but it does mean that we are at least operating in a manner appropriate to the second half of this century.

In moving to a new site we chose a location near a major parkway, providing the most visibility we could afford. Our building plans received an award from the Florida Association of the American Institute of Architects. The structures resulting from these plans are contemporary in appearance, but not so different as to be bizarre. They are a source of pride to the members of the congregation.

Our congregation is the only Unitarian Universalist society in the county. We feel, therefore, that we must appeal to a wide range of both thought and style. It is never wise to attempt to be all things to all people, but it is necessary to be as inclusive as possible within our Unitarian Universalist universe.

Truly, our congregation has been blessed with outstanding leadership. Successive presidents and committee chairpersons have used their authority appropriately. This has allowed us to move cooperatively toward the achievement of our goals.

Perhaps our greatest strength has been the way we have continued to live together as members of a religious community. I am not going to suggest that our congregation is completely without tension and stress. There is disagreement. There is controversy. And, yes, there is occasional acrimony. Our rapid growth has created pains as well as gains.

We strive to treat one another with dignity and respect. Graciousness is actively encouraged. Gratuitous conflict is avoided. A remarkable harmony of spirit has been achieved in the context of a rich diversity of personalities. We believe that congregational experience can enhance the meaning of members' lives by providing nurture and encouragement as well as challenge. For growth to occur, we know that parish life must be pleasant. Few people are attracted to communities rife with conflict, tension, and recrimination. Most people are not actively seeking additional pain and unhappiness.

More than anything else we believe that our free faith flourishes when we truly live out our ideals both individually and institutionally. This means serving one another in community while reaching out to others in hope.

Deeds Speak Louder

John A. Buehrens

I HAVE GOOD NEWS and I have bad news. The good news is that we Unitarian Universalists have a saving message. It is not a new message nor a unique one: Others proclaim it as well. My friend William Sloane Coffin puts it this way in his book *A Passion for the Possible: A Message to US Churches*:

> The chief religious question is not "What must I do to be saved?" but rather, "What must we all do to save God's creation?". . . .[T]he religious community has the saving vision. It is the ancient prophetic vision of human unity, now become an urgent, pragmatic necessity. According to this vision, we all belong to one another, every one of us five and a half billion people on this planet. . . . Human unity is not something we are called on to create, only to recognize and make manifest. . . . Were religious people everywhere to implement the unity they profess, a unity universal and eternal, the future would appear far more promising.

We Unitarian Universalists, who have this vision in our very name, have a particular calling. It is not merely to proclaim the vision. That is easy enough. The bad news is that we are each also called upon to *do* something about it.

Let's face it: Most of us have been blessed beyond our deserving. We are a privileged people. Whatever sufferings any one of us may have encountered, most of us have been blessed with a good education, enough to eat, and opportunities to live useful lives.

Unlike some more metaphysical forms of religion, our faith does not treat evil, sin, and death as unreal. It asks us to pray for lives that are worthy of all the good things that are ours. It challenges us to make our deeds the principal answer to our prayers.

As our own Adlai Stevenson once said, "We travel together, passengers on this little spaceship, dependent on its vulnerable supplies of air and soil; all committed for our safety to its security and peace, preserved from annihilation only by the care, the work, and I will say, the love we give our fragile craft."

None of us can do everything. Each of us is finite. We are each limited in talent, time, money, energy, love, and wisdom— among other things. But each of us can surely do something. We may begin small and self-involved. Humans do. But we are capable of growth, spiritually and morally.

This is the reason for religious communities. In one sense, our form of religious association *is* unique. It recognizes at its very core that the important thing about religious living is not what we profess with our lips but how we witness with our lives. It says that your mother was right: Deeds do speak louder than words.

Not that we need to live alike, much less think alike, in order to love alike. Community does not mean sameness. Your calling is not quite the same as mine. Not in practical work, not in spiritual practice. We often say that ours is a noncreedal community. That is not because we have no beliefs. It is because we will not make words the test of faith, only deeds.

To paraphrase the late A. Powell Davies, belief is many

things, and so is disbelief. But religious lives are lived when we open the mind to greater truth, the heart to greater compassion, and the conscience to the demand of justice.

Most religious groups ask the question, What do we all believe in common? That is the creedal question. The question we ask instead is the covenantal question, What are we willing to *promise* to one another, and to the world?

I agree with Martin Buber's definition of humankind. We are the only animal that is capable of promise-making, promise-breaking, and promise-renewing. The promise that Unitarian Universalism holds is great. In an era when the very fate of the earth itself depends on broad democratic participation in asking the right questions, it dares to explore what those questions are and not to substitute easy or merely traditional answers.

Let me tell you something of my own experience with Unitarian Universalism and its emphasis on "deeds not creeds."

The first congregation I served as minister was in Knoxville, Tennessee. Shortly after I arrived there in 1973, a friend from the North asked me what it was like to be a UU minister in the midst of the Bible Belt. I replied that it was a bit like running a theological decompression chamber for people with the Baptist bends. Freedom is a heady thing. It can cause reverse fundamentalism if all it allows is denial. When the Bible Belt is unbuckled, it can be downright vulgar. My job, I had concluded, was to put us all under a little pressure again. Pressure even from the biblical tradition, reinterpreted less as pat answers and more as centered around some tough questions.

What might be required of us in the way of doing justice in this community? In being agents of love and mercy? In walking more humbly with our neighbors? Only through such pressure, I decided, could some of us get our blood gasses back to normal and show what, if anything, we might be good for. Fortunately, there were plenty of people among the founders of the congregation to serve as good examples of steady faith in action.

They had organized the church in 1949. It was racially integrated from the start, which was unheard of in East Tennessee. Soon they were in the forefront of the civil rights struggle. Even before school desegregation, members developed an interracial summer day camp, where black and white children could play and learn together. Its location had to be kept secret, and changed from time to time, to avoid Klan harassment. Later, many of the sit-ins to desegregate public facilities were planned at the church.

By the mid-1970s, when I arrived, the marches and sit-ins were over. Whites were caught up in the "Me Decade." Separatist pressures in the black community had caused some black leaders to withdraw from the church. Few replacements had come along. Still, it remained, in the words of Wallace Robbins, "a church of moral work, not because morality is a sufficient faith," but because faith without works *is* dead.

My predecessors had developed relationships with a number of low-income families, black and white, living on public assistance or in public housing. Most were disabled in some way. Visiting them and helping in little matters helped put real experience with real people behind new efforts. Becoming active with the local antipoverty effort, the Community Action Committee, I soon chaired its administrative committee. As the large state psychiatric hospital in town began to deinstitutionalize, UUs helped form an interfaith effort to provide group homes. I became a spokesperson for decent care of people with long-term mental illness.

Many, of course, ended up homeless on the streets of our cities. In the early 1980s, when I was minister in Dallas, Texas, I co-chaired a Mayor's Task Force on Homelessness that documented that fact, proposing ways that public policy, and not just private charity, was needed in response.

Religious people do need to work for changes in public policy. Charity is *not* enough. But there are effective and ineffective ways for people of faith to go about working for social justice. In the mid-1980s I served as chair of a task force appointed by the UUA Board of Trustees to study social justice efforts throughout the movement.

What we found was good intentions, but too often gone awry. In the aftermath of the 1960s, a certain disparagement of mere "social service projects" had set in. Few of our congregations had any opportunities for people actually to practice what former UUA President Bill Schulz called a "theology of dirty hands." Too many committees on "social action" had become all talk. Henry might advocate reform of the United Nations; Muriel, saving the Amazon rain forest; George, disarmament; and Mary, ending racism, sexism, and homophobia. The minister might even preach passionately on such themes. Yet one had to wonder how spiritually sound or effective such efforts were.

One could hear it from folks the task force surveyed. Parishioners expressed it. "The church never seems to do anything, just talk," complained some. One said, "I don't like the prevailing tone of anger in what the minister fancies are 'social action' sermons. Playing 'ain't it awful' doesn't move *me* to action." Still others raised the old (and false) dichotomy between social action and spirituality.

In 1987, the task force recommended that the UUA put more emphasis on helping local congregations find their own distinctive vocation in helping to make the world more just, and the methods to do so more effectively.

Here is one testimony as to how it has worked. When Dr. Marilyn Sewell became minister of the First Unitarian Church in Portland, Oregon, she found that, despite a long history of social involvement, many people wanted to "do more" than an existing social action committee seemed able to handle. "I let it die," says Marilyn. "I had to resist propping it up. The committee was part of the problem, not part of the solution. Then we invited Lola Peters from the UUA to come do a workshop for us. She was marvelous. A whole new group of people turned out. They helped identify several areas where we could actually *do* things."

Five task forces were formed. One does projects with and advocacy work on behalf of children in poverty. They coordinate with the UU Service Committee "Promise the Children" campaign. Portland is a downtown church, so another group works on hunger and homelessness in the inner city. They shelter thirty homeless women, house an agency called Transition Projects, and help a neighboring church feed some 2,000 people a month.

After Marilyn asked in a sermon how many would be willing to fast at noon once a week and give the cost of a lunch to the program, over half the congregation did so. Still another task force works on low-income housing, both through Habitat for Humanity and with their own project.

In her own contribution to this volume, Marilyn has written about what was perhaps their best-publicized effort: a huge ribbon, labeling the congregation's buildings a "Hate Free Zone," was tied around a city block.

Meanwhile, the Portland congregation is booming. Three services have to be held each Sunday morning. Over 400 new members have joined. They come, says Marilyn, "not for escape, but for deepening, and for a congregation that connects spirituality to the pain and needs of the world we live in."

Other growing congregations in the UUA are much the same. Social ministry projects are being seen as opportunities not just to change the world, but to change ourselves as well. Unity Church (Unitarian) in St. Paul, Minnesota, began a Center for Spiritual Development as part of its adult religious education program. But the first projects to promote spiritual growth all have to do with opportunities to practice hospitality and service.

Certainly this fits the experience I had myself at the Unitarian Church of All Souls in New York City. First the congregation began a traditional soup kitchen. That seemed impersonal, however; so clients of the Neighborhood Coalition for Shelter were soon being given real hospitality at All Souls on Monday evenings. "Talking with a little compassion to a person who's homeless is good for me," one volunteer told me. "I'm less callous, less despairing myself. We may be only a tiny step toward a solution, but it has also made me more politically active."

One classic analysis says that there are four ways in which a congregation or an individual can try to serve justice: service, education, witness, and political action. I found that a program of congregational social ministry can and should build one on the other in precisely that order.

Service projects should not be disparaged as "mere Band-Aids on open wounds." Perhaps they are that. I sometimes think of soup kitchens and shelters as an irresponsible state exploiting the church. Yet in every community there are people in need. Religious people, to be responsible, must try to respond—for the sake of their own souls. A good program of congregational social ministry creates hands-on opportunities for spiritual growth through service to others.

On that broad base, social education can't help but take place. People begin to ask, Why does this problem exist? What changed social policies would best help? At a certain point, people at All Souls began working with children in one of the city's notorious welfare hotels. "Who owns this hell hole?" they asked. South African investors, they learned. Each of the 300 rooms held a whole family and cost over $1,500 a month. "Why not put our tax dollars into fixing abandoned apartment buildings for low-income families?" they asked.

Soon we came to the public witness phase. Joining with an Interfaith Coalition on Housing and Homelessness, hundreds of members turned out at a rally at City Hall to demand new policies. One member, Sylvia Ann Hewlett, was inspired to write a book, *When the Bough Breaks: The Cost of Neglecting America's Children*. Because we were doing something, people listened.

Finally, a group of attorneys in the congregation investigated laws promoting public-private cooperation in renovating housing for families. The trustees were challenged to invest a portion of the church's endowment in a revolving loan fund. Other churches and synagogues were asked to pitch in. Last I heard, over 400 apartments had been completed! And one All Souls member played a leading role in getting Congress to pass laws to help finance such projects.

Deeds Speak Louder

During the first five years that I served at All Souls, the congregation grew by over fifty percent, from 900 to nearly 1,400 members. The number of social ministry projects expanded to over twenty, involving as many as 800 volunteers. A nationally recognized AIDS Task Force combined one-to-one lay ministry, support groups, home-delivered meals, and public education. (Their early posters in the buses and subways said, "AIDS is a human disease and deserves a humane response," and "Treat a person with AIDS with kindness. It won't kill you.")

Another project involved "adopting" a low-income public elementary school. We encouraged teachers, provided volunteers, increased parent involvement, supported an after-school program of arts, theater, and enrichment, and helped overcome neglect by school authorities. Similar projects are under way by UU congregations in Atlanta, Georgia; West Hartford, Connecticut; Rockford, Illinois; and elsewhere.

We also formed a Partner Church relationship with a small, predominantly African American UCC congregation in East Harlem. Letting them take the lead, we worked on a learning center for children, a study group on Africa for adults, shared worship, and an interfaith partnership to fight racial and ethnic tension. The Partnership of Faith in New York City, with a UU minister as executive director, brings together some 200 religious leaders and their congregations—Protestant, Catholic, UU, Jewish, Muslim, and others—the broadest such group in the city's history.

The best news in the Unitarian Universalist Association, from my new perspective as president, is that all across the continent our congregations are getting involved in social ministry. The models vary, but often they go beyond delegating everything to a social action committee. Task forces and projects abound. Best of all, while activity has increased, polarization around ideology has diminished.

There is a simple reason for this. What we are doing is an expression of faith. Years ago I asked Rabbi Levi Olan for advice on religion and politics. He was a great and prophetic spiritual leader. During the civil rights struggle and the Vietnam era, he became known in Dallas as "the conscience of the city." Levi replied, "Study the prophets. Preach prophetic religion. Practice such religion. Political consequences, people can judge for themselves."

I think Levi was right. As Bill Coffin notes, "An old saying holds that religion and politics don't mix. Probably it was first said by Pharaoh when he turned down Moses' plea to 'let my people go.' Generally what it means is, 'Your religion doesn't mix with my politics.'"

Still, a noncreedal church is not called to substitute a political orthodoxy for a theological one. It isn't even called upon to provide must-be-believed answers, either metaphysical or political. It is simply called to live in the deep questions.

Some are as ancient as Micah's. Some are as modern as Coffin's. It does not matter if we do not all agree on just what we must do if we find we have different callings that emphasize a variety of smaller questions. To keep faith with our noncreedal, covenantal approach to religion, all we need do is keep living in the big and enduring questions: What are we willing to promise one another, and the world? What are we doing to fulfill and renew those promises? What are we doing to demonstrate our faith in human unity and our love for this universe?

The promise in Unitarian Universalism is great indeed—greater than our relatively small numbers would indicate. We have always had an impact far larger than mere numbers would explain. Whenever we have grown numerically and institutionally, I think the reasons are simple: because we have grown spiritually, because we have behaved well, because we have remembered that it is not our words that count. Our deeds do indeed speak louder.

May the witness that arises from lives well lived and deeds well done continue to strengthen our faith in the years ahead, that the promise in Unitarian Universalism may yet be fulfilled.

Spirituality and Church Growth

Arvid Straube

Breathing in, I am a mountain.
Breathing out, I feel solid.

Breathing in, I am space.
Breathing out, I feel free.

IT IS A THURSDAY EVENING and thirty men and women are sitting cross-legged on the floor or in chairs engaging together in the ancient meditation practice of following the breath. In order to help keep their attention on the breath, they silently repeat the couplets developed by Vietnamese Zen master Thich Nhat Hanh to assist anxious and scattered modern Western minds to settle into the calm focus of meditation.

This group is but one of the groups that meets weekly, monthly or more than monthly for the explicit purpose of developing the spiritual growth of its participants. There is a Men's Support Group, a Friday Morning Meditation Group, a Hatha Yoga group, the Wednesday Night Minister's Class, a Parenting Class, a Spiritual Autobiography Class, a New Physics Class, a Neo-Pagan group, and several Women's Spi-

Spirituality and Church Growth

rituality groups. In addition there are Saturday workshops, such as Living with Awareness and Compassion, Spirituality in the Workplace, and Chinese Medicine. Old classes finish and new ones are begun, sometimes by the program staff of the church, sometimes by volunteers.

In the ten years between 1983 and 1993, the Eno River Unitarian Universalist Fellowship in Durham, North Carolina, which I serve as senior minister, grew from 172 to 560. Our average attendance at two Sunday morning services has surpassed 400. Our tremendous growth is due to several factors. We are in a prime location, situated in a rapidly developing area between Durham and Chapel Hill, North Carolina. The rapid growth of the area is demographically suited for potential Unitarian Universalists. Many people are finding this a good area in which to retire. We have one of the best, most comprehensive religious education programs for children and youth, who often lead their educated, baby-boomer parents to church. These are all factors that get people here. I think they stay, in large part, for more amorphous, less specific reasons. They are expressed in various ways. Often reasons center around the word "spirituality."

It seems to me that most churches in this country attempt to provide for what church leaders think ought to be people's religious needs. These leaders do a poor job of listening to and providing what the multitudes, both churched and unchurched, themselves perceive as their religious needs. Often what church leaders feel ought to be people's religious needs tend to be those things that fit the needs of the institutional church, such as identification with a particular denomination and a particular congregation, a sense of stewardship, and a willingness to offer time and talent within the organized activities of the church. We tend to look for people who will fit into the slots we have prepared for them, in churches where the basic emphasis has not changed since the fifties. When people do not flock to our empty pews we can always blame the individualism and consumer mentality of our culture.

Often in Unitarian Universalist congregations we offer those seekers who visit us the same fare that was offered in the fifties—a scientific humanism that called into question the religious traditions and theological language of the vast majority of our neighbors. We still operate far too often on the assumption that the best we have to offer is an intellectual critique of traditional religion and a prescription for living based on the sovereignty of reason. When I was last in the search process in the early eighties, all of the packets I looked at had the congregation rate "intellectual stimulation" as by far the top factor they were looking for in sermons. This is probably still true. But I think it is true only because the real top reason isn't one of the choices. Why are there not items like "increasing integrity and wholeness" or "feeding the soul"? These, I feel, are the real hungers that people are bringing to the church today.

The baby boom generation is trying to come back to church. They are being led by their children—by the need to provide them with some kind of religious or moral basis for living. The more conservative among them, we are told by sociologists of religion, are finding their way into the newer, no-name-brand evangelical "centers," "fellowships," and mega-churches. The less conservative may have tried the mainline churches of their childhood again, but have been turned off by these denominations' lack of ability to change with the times. These are the ones who identified with the anti-war and civil rights movements, and who were greened by the greening of America. They may have experimented with LSD and other psychedelic drugs and quite likely smoked marijuana and inhaled. They read Alan Watts, Baba Ram Dass, and Carlos Casteneda. They were the counterculture, and in the nineties, with children of their own and careers in the establishment, are aware that the spiritual yearnings they turned eastward and inward to satisfy in the sixties are still there.

Being a good earner and consumer is suddenly not enough. The questions come with greater urgency as midlife approaches. Am I doing good as well as doing well? Am I being the example

Spirituality and Church Growth

I need to be to my children? What will my life mean when I'm no longer here on this planet? How can I love well? How can I heal my deep psychic wounds? How can I live my daily life with compassion, awareness, morality, and integrity? How can I reach out past my isolation and experience meaningful communion with others? These are all profoundly spiritual questions, questions more of the heart than the head. Unlike the traditional potential convert of Unitarian Universalism of past decades, these people tend not to be fresh refugees from more orthodox religion. They do not need to rebel. They did their rebelling in the sixties. They are not looking for a refuge from Methodism but from secularism, hedonism, and consumerism.

So, what is this spirituality that people nowadays seem to be looking for more than anything else from our churches? The *American Heritage Dictionary* defines "spiritual" as "of, relating to, consisting of, or having the nature of spirit; not tangible or material," and "of, concerning with, or affecting the soul." This "not tangible or material" essence of the spiritual is the reason people cannot say with any precision what they mean when they use the word "spirituality." Our culture is overly concerned with the tangible and material. We are in danger of defining the nature of the human soul purely in materialistic terms. But so many of the most important aspects of our lives simply cannot be measured in material terms. The origin of the word "spiritual" is from the Latin *spiritus*, meaning breath. The breath cannot be seen with the naked eye, but its existence cannot be questioned. So it is with other aspects of life, such as love, kindness, hope, faith, compassion, determination, humor, loyalty, patience, self-restraint, and cheerfulness. They cannot exist outside of individuals who exhibit them, but they are very real, and life would be unbearable without them.

One important aspect of spirituality is relationship. I like to define a person's spirituality as one's relationships to the unseen sources of support for one's existence. This definition includes within it our relationship to nature, with other human beings, to our ancestors, and to the deep sources of strength within and all about us. These latter sources have been named "God" in our culture. The word "God" is much less problematic to the boomer seekers in our churches than it may have been to previous generations of potential Unitarian Universalists. Many in those previous generations felt that it was necessary to reject 4,000 years of Western spirituality based on the Bible. The boomers do not share this "allergy" to traditional theological language. They are thirsty for spirit from whatever source, and they are impatient with rigidity and intolerance in whatever guise. Although they reject the rigidity of the mainline and evangelical churches, they are very interested in their spiritual roots and are confused and put off if, on visiting a Unitarian Universalist congregation, they are told that, "We don't use the word 'God' here." The minister needs to feel free to preach from whatever systems of language and belief feed his or her own spiritual vision. Boomers are comfortable with and eager for spiritual food from sources ancient and modern, eastern and western.

Spiritual preaching is the core of the program for congregations who wish to take seriously the spiritual needs of current and prospective members. Spiritual preaching is preaching that comes from the preachers own spiritual struggles and relationship with God. It is preaching, as Emerson reminds us, that is the preacher's life, passed through the fires of his or her thought. Such traditional UU sermons as the lengthy book review, the quote-filled essay, or the cerebral discussion of a current issue will leave potential boomer congregants cold. The topics that will really engage the visitor and new member in the spiritual church are those that touch on the life questions referred to above, that brought them to seek a spiritual community in the first place.

In order to preach effectively in this mode, the preacher needs to view the nurture of his or her own spiritual life as the most important ongoing preaching task. Most of us enter the ranks of the clergy because, as laypersons, we have seen in the life of the church and its concerns at least the potential for realizing the larger dimensions of life. We hunger to realize this "life more abundant" for ourselves and to help others realize it as well. So we are called to the ministry. It is a spiritual quest, the mystical hero's journey, upon which we wish to embark. But with seminary, internship, and early settlements we find that the work of the church, like any other work in our society, threatens to be overcome, not by the spiritual but by the tangible and material. It revolves around committees and task forces, budgets and staffing. The need for comfort and support by congregants is inexhaustible, and too often we as clergy think we need to do it all. Perhaps our compassion and care is overtaxed. Time pressures mount, and life becomes ever-more frantic. In responding to the loud voices from all sides, there is one voice that is ignored—the still, small voice within, the voice of our spiritual hunger. What irony, that the one who was called to a spiritual quest has no time for prayer, meditation, and spiritual reading!

When there is no time for the minister's own spiritual prac-tice, the insights dry up. The preacher becomes the retailer of the spiritual insights of others rather than a model of a vital spiritual life. The preaching comes more and more from the head and less and less from the heart. It becomes spiritual stone and not spiritual bread. The nurture of the minister's own spiritual life ideally would consist of fifteen to thirty minutes daily of meditation or prayer, a monthly meeting with a spiritual director, and regular meetings with a group of peers in which the minister does not have leadership responsibility. Annual or semi-annual spiritual retreats of at least a week are valuable as well.

After the nurture of the minister's own spiritual life, the choice of topics is the next most important consideration of spiritual preaching. Here, a creative tension exists between the minister's own spiritual interests and energy and the needs that are suggested by the struggles of members of the congregation. This is not just a matter of "give 'em what they want" preach-ing. Most baby boomers would rather never hear a sermon on giving and stewardship, but every spiritual tradition that I am aware of insists that the cultivation of generosity is absolutely necessary for spiritual growth. The call to serve others is universal as well.

Boomers yearn to serve and share. Many, however, have not the slightest idea on how to go about it. They tend not to like the traditional UU approach of exhaustive analysis of a social problem followed by letters to the editor, to legislators, or perhaps the drafting of a General Assembly resolution. They do not see themselves as "engaging in social action." They see themselves as wanting to share and to serve. This too is part of the spiritual quest, for the spiritual worldview insists that we are one with all humanity and with the earth. Our relationship with each other and to the earth is inseparable from spiritual practice. This does not mean that we will never write letters, but there is a pronounced preference for "hands-on" kinds of service.

At Eno River we have participated with an African American Lutheran church in sponsoring race relations dialogues for the larger community, have built a house for a family sponsored by Habitat for Humanity, and are engaged in a tutoring program for children at risk and a remodeling of the local battered women's shelter. We have also taken our turn at providing food for the soup kitchen and have gleaned harvested fields to supply the soup kitchen and the food bank. For the last two years, we have had a "canvass check off" in which those canvassed are offered the opportunity to add a small amount to their church pledge to fund a major community service project. Such direct service has been criticized as not being radical enough and addressing only the symptoms of a problem and not the underlying inequities of our system. I answer these criticisms with the observation that direct contact with the oppressed in our society has radicalized more people than a hundred sermons. A huge portion of our congregation is or has been directly involved in one of these projects. Many find it the most rewarding part of their lives.

In addition to preaching and service, an essential part of the program dedicated to the spiritual growth of its members is a broad and varied adult religious education program. What is needed is a wide variety of classes, workshops, and support groups to equip people for their spiritual journeys. Using the definition of spirituality as our relationship to those unseen forces underlying our existence, we can divide these offerings into relationships with others (children, parents, partners, and co-workers), relationship to the deeper parts of the self (one's work; one's religious past; one's thoughts, motives, feelings, and dreams), and one's relationship with God, The Source, The Universe. Although the Unitarian Universalist Association has a wide variety of good and not so good curricula for adult religious education, I strongly recommend that a congregation develop as much as possible its own groups and classes, suitable to the needs of their particular community. We have found this to be richly rewarding.

UUA curricula tend to favor the eight- to twelve-session, two-hour evening model. A limited number of people in our busy, two working-parent society are able to commit themselves to that many Tuesday or Wednesday nights in a row. I suggest experimentation with different formats. We have an ongoing Wednesday night class, preceded by an inexpensive catered dinner and accompanied by child care, which is on a strictly drop-in basis. This has been taught by the senior minister who varies the topics as seems appropriate. It has been very successful. We have also been very successful with one-time, all-day Saturday or Sunday afternoon workshops and with a morning adult Sunday school class. Space does not permit us to expand the latter idea.

When you do offer an eight- to twelve-week class, see if people might want to continue meeting for another eight to twelve weeks to continue pursuing their interest. Look closely at who might be a natural leader for the group and groom him or her to take over the leadership of the group. It is likely that after the second eight- to twelve-week session, the group will continue on an indefinite basis. It is well known in church administration literature that churches with more than 150 at Sunday morning worship need to meet the intimacy needs of members in small face-to-face groups. At that point the member-ship is too large for everyone to feel known and cared for in the group as a whole. It is through membership in an ongoing group that the intimacy and belonging needs of members are met. It is important to keep in mind that new members are much more comfortable in new rather than existing groups, so one should make the most of any opportunity to create a new ongoing group.

Involving the general membership, in addition to the staff, as faculty for adult religious education is vital if the church is to generate the necessary number of programs. In any congregation of midsize and up, there will be members who are quite advanced in particular areas of spiritual knowledge and spiritual develop-ment techniques. In our congregation we have had a yoga instruc-tor, a nationally recognized amateur Merton scholar, an acu-puncturist, a serious student of the new physics, and several psychotherapists offer workshops and classes. After a while the adult religious education leadership gets the knack of keeping their "ear to the ground" for those opportunities.

I have found the "instant workshop" formula to be quite useful as well. No experts are needed for this at all. The partici-pants become the experts. Put an invitation in the newsletter and other congregational media asking members to meet about a particular concern. The workshop leader convenes the group for a few hours on a Saturday morning and asks each member how they relate to the concern. Then the leader asks if anyone present has ideas, experiences, or knowledge that will address the con-cerns of anyone else. The ideas can be collected and later presented to the congregation in a newsletter article. We have successfully addressed the topics of meaningful Christmas cel-ebrations and of dealing with close family members hostile to Unitarian Universalism through this method.

It should go without saying that a strong program for children and youth is essential for keeping the interest and loyalty of baby boom members. Ours is well run and very good. The adult religious education leadership supplements this emphasis with parenting classes and seminars on particular parenting issues such as attention deficit disorder. The opportunity must exist for the spiritual growth of adults as well as children in the congregation that seeks to support people on their spiritual journeys.

I think that providing men, women, and children with a community of support for spiritual growth and healing is some of the most urgent and important work on the planet. It is countercultural as well in a society that devalues the unseen and is obsessed with the material and tangible. In the sense that vast parts of the self are restored to the person who discovers the spiritual dimensions of life, it is no exaggeration to say that it is a matter of the saving of souls.

The Church as a Network of Study, Service, and Social Groups

Brent A. Smith

WE LIVE IN A TIME of cultural contradiction. On the one hand there is evidence of a deep spiritual longing. Many people do not live in the town of their upbringing and yearn for the "rootedness" that familiarity of place and familial connection gave previous generations. Loneliness, purposelessness, and meaninglessness characterize many lives (see Shawchuck and Rath, *Marketing Congregations*). Over ninety percent of Americans say they believe in God, with some researchers putting the number as high as ninety-eight percent. More than half say they pray once a day. Yet, paradoxically, people as a general rule do not turn to institutional religion to deal with these issues. The percentage of the US population that attends church hovers around forty-five percent, whereas a recent "pew count" in major denominations yielded a surprisingly low twenty-eight percent!

This is a fundamental shift from generations past who found the church to be the central institution in their lives (see Callahan, *Twelve Keys to the Effective Church*). It's called the shift from a "churched" to an "unchurched" culture. Even in the Bible Belt where I am pastor of a church, most educators and ministers are appalled by the lack of general literacy concerning religion, especially Christianity. In the minds of many, the church, like other institutions in our culture, emerged from the 1960s as a source of suspicion. Many claim it is only after their money and is not relevant to their lives. With the characteristics mentioned above, it is clear that in the non-church-going public, which comprises the vast majority of Americans, almost all churches are lumped together as insensitive, uncaring bastions of pietism (with, surprisingly enough, no theological distinctions having been made). In other words, now, in the minds of the majority in our country, a church is a church is a church, be it Unitarian or Episcopal or Presbyterian. "They aren't for me," it's often said or thought, "because they are not relevant to my world or sensitive to my needs."

Yet, a spiritual yearning persists. Social critic Michael Lerner in the magazine *Tikkun* (vol. 7, #4, p.5) sums it up this way:

> Most Americans are in deep pain about their lives. They face stress and alienation at work and often find it difficult to maintain friendships and keep families together. They are haunted by the sense that their children are growing up without any moral foundation, and a sense that their lives are isolated, directionless, and without larger purpose and meaning. All these feelings are typically refracted through the dominant meritocratic ideologies of American society so that most Americans become enmeshed in a deep process of self-blaming. As a result, many Americans feel terrible about themselves and find themselves in need of some way to cover up their pain and depression.

The thesis of this chapter is that the free church can respond to this spiritual hunger in part through the creation and maintenance of small groups devoted to study, service, and social functions. This model of church structure, called the "meta-church," has been used by the fastest growing evangelical Christian congregations as a way for the institution of the church to confront this spiritual hunger given the cultural conditions we now face. The model of small groups is not foreign to the free church; perhaps the most famous "intentional small group" in our history was the Transcendental Club, whose purpose included the learned investigation of religion and revelation. The Free Religious Association, the "Unity Men," even the Fellowship Movement were attempts to wed fellowship, inquiry, and service under the disciplines of the free church tradition. The "meta-church" structure of small groups may not be foreign to us, but neither has the free church understood its dynamics in growing large church communities.

Small groups are not just a particular component of the meta-church, but a way of conceiving of the entire community. A church becomes a network of many small groups. Currently, there are three dimensions of church structure in which my church is seeking to implement the meta-church model as we grow into such a network: study (adult education), service (social concerns and church volunteer work), and social (fellowship). Each serves a unique function in addressing our culture's spiritual hunger.

At All Souls Unitarian Church in Tulsa, Oklahoma, we are convinced that one of the main purposes of religious institutions is educational. This is especially true in light of the culture's current religious illiteracy. In our Roots classes (for newcomers) it is not surprising to find eighty to ninety percent totally ignorant of the origin and meaning of the Apostles' Creed. Simple biblical knowledge is lacking, let alone any reasoned critique of world religions. No wonder meaninglessness is identified as a characteristic of the "unchurched" culture! Whereas twenty years ago most people arrived in the free church having escaped an oppressive experience in a previous church, most today are arriving uninformed about what religion and churches are, with nominal recent church experience. And so our purposes with new people these days are less therapeutic and more educational, less convincing them their negative responses were justifiable and more building understanding about religion in general and loyalty to free religion in particular. Thus, it becomes our responsibility to teach the history and ideas of the covenental, free church in order to help provide an adequate framework for meaning in a person's life. This we do through involvement in small groups devoted to study.

Characteristic of an "unchurched" culture, people arrive in churches looking for deeper purposes to their lives. They may have experienced a deepening sense of social duty through the "activist climate" of the 1960s. But, they may also have become somewhat cynical in realizing "not much has changed." Hence, they want a difference they can feel, not just send money to. They want to make a tangible difference. Our small service groups give them a way. We divide these groups into two focuses: those that help the church function (ushering, building repair, calling on the elderly, etc.) and those that help society function (including currently at our church, building a house for a Habitat for Humanity family, volunteering in the elementary school we have adopted, working on one of our AIDS Care Teams, serving a meal at the homeless shelter, etc.). These are not "one shot" deals, but ongoing small groups whose function is to provide tangible service opportunities with a group bonding experience. People derive purpose through small groups devoted to service.

Finally, people come to church lonely. They are wary enough of churches to want to remain anonymous on Sunday morning while they are "shopping." Yet, they've come for connections of some sort and, surprisingly enough, care less about what theology a church promulgates than whether their relational needs can be met. This is what church athletic teams, neighborhood groups, circle suppers do. Although fellowship is a component of all small groups, there are many people who care less about explicitly religious concerns. The loneliness characteristic of the "unchurched" culture is abetted through involvement in small groups devoted to social functions.

All of these small groups have similar structures, rules, and guidelines. Notice they are not committees or boards, which really are the main ways that longer standing members contribute to the life of the community. Yet, the responsibilities of both lay and clergy need to be well defined and adhered to.

Structurally, each small group area, study, service, and social, is likened to a pyramid. Laity lead the small groups, but each small group leader is chosen and trained by professional staff, because it is imperative that the purposes of the free church be communicated and fulfilled in the small group. It is the responsibility of clergy to train leaders and write curricula and gather materials to be used in the small group, but clergy do not lead the groups. The leader of a small group, in conjunction with the minister, chooses an assistant, who eventually will function as a leader of a group. A hospitality person is chosen who takes care of many group needs, including recognition of birthdays, special events in the lives of people, and so forth. The leader of each group watches over the spiritual development of each member and meets frequently with the minister and other leaders for spiritual development to discuss problems, challenges, and instances where a response from the minister is needed (hospitalization, death of a family member, a crisis of faith, etc.).

Guidelines for each group are the same. Groups meet regularly; no more than once per week and certainly no less than once per month. Each group produces a covenant, which includes what each person hopes to get out of the group, what gifts each brings to the group, and the recognition that the group is part of the larger church community. At All Souls we communicate to our new people the expectation that they serve the community for at least one year. We steer new people to service through study, which they find intriguing and easy to fulfill. Hence, over five years' time, a church can "grow" a community that includes the expectation of service, with a variety of choices to fulfill that. Two rules for small group formation are essential to the health of the entire community and are a particular challenge in the free church. First, every small group must be consciously related to the larger church community and the larger body's central exaltation of shared values, that is, the worship service. Without this necessary link, small groups can easily become "mini-churches" with purposes different, and sometimes contrary, to the community itself. At All Souls we do this through a simple, small group ritual: the sharing in opening/closing words, prayers, and other repeated phrases and wordings that are commonly used during corporate worship. Again, though, it is not ritual that the small group itself comes to generate, because it is not the function of small groups to create the values and vision expressed by the entire community.

Second, each small group must include as part of its purpose the intentional creation of another small group. It must have a mission beyond itself, by spawning another group. Without this mission, the small group can too easily become simply a group that "takes care of its own," which will eventually defeat the purposes of the larger community. Again, this rule is hard for those in the free church, who often like to cluster in closed groups as part of a way to create identity. Each participant in a small group must understand that bringing someone new to the small group, to experience what he or she has, is fulfilling the mission of the larger church to maintain and extend religious freedom. Wherever free churches implement meta-church principles, they will face growth both in numbers and depth of community. This is because many in the culture so desperately need what small group involvement in a free church can bring and because the experience itself will help shape people into persons who understand and covet the traditions and ideas of religious freedom.

To Grow a Serving Church

Susan Milnor

MY CO-MINISTER AND SPOUSE, Terry Sweetser, once shared an office with a clinical psychologist. The psychologist watched many of Terry's ministerial antics with curiosity, but he was most bemused by the summer schedule. "How important is what you do in that church if you can afford to shut down for three months?" he asked.

Surely the issue of summer cool down is more complex than his question presupposes. Still, it reveals our own dismissive attitude toward the work of our churches. Indeed, in my experience, although some longer term members like the tradition of gearing down in the summer, most newer members are puzzled or dismayed by it. As we have expanded the services and programs offered during the summer at First Universalist Church of Minneapolis, congregational involvement and expectation have risen.

The work we do in our Unitarian Universalist congregations should be so important that we cannot turn it off for months or even weeks. If we want to build communities that transform people's lives, we must take our programs and services—and the importance they can have—seriously. It might seem strange to think of providing quality programming as a means of spreading the "good news" of our faith, but in fact it is one of the most powerful means of evangelizing we have. People are drawn to a faith that inspires commitment. To go further, it is even a theological matter. If we truly believe that every person is of great worth and value, if we believe that God is manifest in us all, we will try to embody that belief in the way we treat people in our own communities.

The growth we have had at First Universalist Church in Minneapolis serves as a good illustration. In five and a half years, our adult membership has risen from 530 to nearly a thousand, our church school from 250 to more than 500. During this time *we* undertook no intentional programs for growth, and we did negligible advertising. Nor did the wider congregation have any vision of growing. In fact, a vocal element clearly did not want the church to become larger. What we set about doing was to create a "full-service," celebrative religious community and to do it as well as we possibly could. The growth happened because of the broadening and deepening of congregational life.

To be "full service" means to provide opportunities for members and friends to develop spiritually, to grow emotionally, to participate in efforts to make the world more just, to find God, to mark the great passages of life, and to create and celebrate the "beloved community." Many of us require a critical shift in our thinking, however, before we can even conceptualize the full-service church. For many years, I believed our churches should offer only programming that people could not get elsewhere: specifically religious programming. In particular we should not try to do what others could do better. What I did not recognize is simply this: People want to come to their churches for help and development because it is a "safe" and accepting context. If things go wrong, they can come to someone they know. If things go well, they can influence future programming. In our church, we now have three women's support groups and a waiting list, as well as groups for men, multicultural families, people in work transition, and so forth. We are also offering our first partners' enrichment retreat, a program that underlines why it is so important to provide experiences in our communities. Most marriage enrichment programs include only people who are legally married and are not welcoming to people who are of same-sex orientation.

Virtually all of these programs have come into being to meet specifically articulated needs of the congregation. The people in our communities will tell us how to serve them, if only we will listen and see. Whether it is supportive programming for youth, enriching programming for "third agers" (seniors), or any other kind, the mission is not simply practical. There is a greater mandate here. It is, finally, to create in our communities small worlds operating with the values and ethics we wish so fervently for the larger world.

In other words, programming becomes a ministry: a way of reaching out to people, helping them to heal, giving them access to the life-affirming hope of Unitarian Universalism. In an exciting extension experiment, our church has taken on a third minister this year, who has the integration of new members as one of her major charges. She sees adult programming as a key, and her work resulted in more than 100 adult education opportunities for the winter/spring. What a feast of possibilities for the hungry to taste!

What matters most in this situation, however, is developing the affiliate life of our congregation so that all its members have a chance to belong, for we are talking about nothing less than belonging. If we see too many people pass through the revolving door, it is not because our religion is anemic; it is not because they "get over" their need for religion and move on to greater, more secular things. They leave because we do not create the right opportunity for them to come to belong to our faith and for it to belong to them. I often tell prospective members that they will know they are ready to join our congregation when they start saying "we" instead of "they" or "you"—in other words, when they belong in their hearts. Thoughtful, committed programming is a ministry to those who yearn to say "we" instead of "they."

Underlying all of this is the fabric of what it means to be a full-service church. Something wonderful can happen in the living of our public life, something that knits us into the beloved community. When it happens, when a moment transforms "they" into "we," it seems mysterious. And in a way it is. Yet many other moments of preparing and receiving that public life are crucial to its being realized. If we want those moments of nearly mystical bonding, then we must attend to the everyday details. We must ask about virtually everything: Does the way we do this build community or does it impede community? When you start to grapple with that, you get some surprises. Take just one example. People often identify the announcement period in the worship service as one of the most important community-building events. Leave aside that others hate the announcements, and just ask yourself whether the way your congregation makes them builds community. When we looked at this in our church a few years ago, we discovered that people frequently failed to introduce them-selves or others adequately; they often spoke too softly for those in the back to hear; and all of us used acronyms only a veteran could understand, for example, UUA, AUW.

Each instance sounds small in and of itself, but taken together they form a fabric that excludes people, or at least shows a disturbing indifference to their comfort and understanding. In the case of our announcements, visitors and short-timers felt lost. Once we thought of holding a summer service in the lovely park across from our church. We thought of gathering by the creek and sitting in the grass; it would have been great fun. Then, we paused to consider our older members and those with limited mobility. They would not have been able to negotiate the terrain with any ease. Was our message to them, "Stay home this Sunday morning. There is no church for you."? Was that acceptable, or had our priorities grown confused? In spite of the desire to be creative, we determined that our service had to include everyone, leaving the park for another event at another time.

We can more easily see how the big things become matters of service. The little things, the details, are also critically important, however, in creating the kind of community that reaches out and embraces people rather than pushing them away with implicit indifference. What I want to suggest is that an ethic of helpfulness and hospitality is a key to effective evangelism. Each event discussed above says something about Unitarian Universalists in that they are done in our name, by us. It does no good to talk about caring for people all over the world if we are rude to those who come through our doorway. It does no good to dream about including targeted minorities if we cannot make those in our own parlor feel at home. Hospitality is so little, yet so much. Consider just what happens between staff and members, friends and visitors on Sunday morning.

Some time ago our staff began to notice how often we were responding to people's questions by saying, "I don't know." This was especially true on Sundays, when we felt rushed and stressed. Even worse, we sometimes said, "That's not really my area," as if to disavow any responsibility to help them. They surely heard not our good intentions, but the message that we did not have time for them. Aware now of this dynamic, we have tried to curb our instincts and change our practices. Our goal is to know as many of the answers as possible, and, when we do not know, to say, "I will find out for you"; "X can help you, and she or he is at a table in the southwest corner of the social hall"; "Please come with me; we'll find out"; or "I'll take this for you and make certain it gets to the right person."

Among ourselves we sometimes talk of "customer service," but the issue really goes deeper. Isn't the ethic of helpfulness related to our theology, to our belief in the worth and value of every person and a world in which relatedness is sacred? Don't we want those who come into our community, whether for a morning or a lifetime, to feel there is at least one place in their lives where their needs and their contributions matter, where they will be respected and cared for? If so, then we need to try to live that, moment to moment, the best we can.

To Grow a Serving Church

This also means that staff, leaders, and those in charge acknowledge responsibilities we would like sometimes to deny. Recently, our Sunday morning services were being disrupted by babies crying loudly. It was very distracting for many people, including parents who look forward to at least one hour a week of peace and concentration. It is easy enough to be self-righteous about a situation like this, and many people wanted someone to come down hard on the parents of the crying children. When this surfaced in a staff meeting, though, my co-minister made an interesting observation: "We are the ones who have failed here because we have not provided a place those parents can take their babies and still hear the service. People expect that in a church this size, and it is an appropriate expectation." Two weeks later we had speakers working in the foyer outside the sanctuary, as well as benches for people to sit on. We are now investigating the cost of providing a video monitor as well. This may not solve the "crying problem" to everyone's satisfaction, but so far the people who have taken their children out have felt grateful, rather than ashamed or guilty or resentful. We hope that nearly everyone feels served. Surely, it is the responsibility of the community at least to try to solve the problem in a win-win way that helps us all.

Is such an ethic of helpfulness and hospitality dangerous? Can it make our religion too easy, too nice? I don't think so. Attending to our attitude, our implicit messages, and our tone in this way reveals strong commitment to our religion. If we learn anything from the research on vibrant, growing churches, it is that they ask ever-increasing commitment from people. That commitment comes in many forms: giving money, time and talent, making church a priority, caring for its people. We need to remember that our actions and our words embody our values and our theology. If the message of Unitarian Universalism is true, we must articulate it in the best way possible. If our worship, our service, our community building are worth doing, they are worth doing as well as possible. If we really believe in each person's worth and in the sacred quality of community, we will not waste people's time, nor will we treat them with the disrespect of saying, "They won't care about that." Someone will care. The question is whether *we* care.

That brings us to the other major element in a "full-service" church, equally if not more important than the ethic of helping and hospitality. Our communities must celebrate life. In this case, "celebrate" also means mourn and grieve and contemplate when life evokes more sober feelings. But the point is that we must not simply analyze life; we must respond to it, act in it, call forth from it. We must not simply talk about what it would be like to do this or that; we must do it. We must not only admire art and music from afar; we must make them in our midst. Because, you see, if people out there want and need anything, they need and want that celebrative life. They long for it. In many cases, they are starved for it in a world that has little use for spiritual concerns.

That's why the cornerstone of a serving church is what we do on Sunday morning. Usually, people come first to a worship service. It is the very embodiment of the Unitarian Universalism with which we first reach out to people. When we have been in a congregation for years, we forget it, but for newcomers, everything in the service reveals something about us: not just the words spoken, but the way they are spoken; not just the music played, but the way it is received; not just the message articulated, but the relationship among people present as well. Furthermore, Sunday morning is the realization of the beloved community in its most literal form. For these reasons, the services must be created with great care and regarded as an opportunity to serve.

Take sermons, for example. There can almost always be a pastoral element to sermons, if we think of them not only as prophecy, or perspective, but also as service. They should be geared toward dealing with real problems of real people in the real world. That means preachers constantly have to listen to members and friends and consider what they are struggling with, what they care about, what they need. Few things make a preacher feel better than having someone say, "You were talking right to me today"—because then we know that we have served and we have helped to weave the web of community. That service, in turn, becomes evangelism of our Unitarian Universalist message, for these are the sermons people tell their friends about, send to their families, and bring people to hear. This does not mean sermons must always guide people to self-help or be fun to hear. In the long run, truly challenging sermons, which set out our prejudices and social failings and call us into action, deepen the bonds we share as a community of thinking, acting people. Even those classically prophetic sermons, however, must start where people are in their intellectual, moral, and emotional lives.

It's not only what we do that matters. The way we do it also functions as outreach. To talk about this risks sounding as though we are trying to turn out a "product." Still, in reality the attention, understanding, and ability with which we do our services affects people deeply. Take music programs, for example. Our congregation has long valued the music made in its midst, and with growth, this program has flourished. We now have eleven volunteer groups who provide music on Sunday morning, representing a real diversity of genres: jazz group, madrigal singers, flute choir, women's chorus, men's chorus, and so forth. All these groups provide affinity for members, but something more spiritual happens as well. Their work becomes an expression of the joy or sorrow in which we all share. It becomes a way to affirm life, to celebrate being human, being alive, and being in community.

Twice this year an intergenerational orchestra made up of adults and young people from our congregation played in our services. Some of its players were parent and son or daughter. For them, making music together in religious community provided a unique kind of bonding. But their work together also deeply moved the congregation. Adults and youth joining together in the larger celebration of the community gave real-world expression to our ideals. To newcomers, we were saying,

"We don't just talk about youth and adults coming together. We bring them here to make something beautiful."

In this experience, the music joined with other aspects of the service, such as liturgy and sermon, to serve an end that was greater than each element in and of itself. And, although our church's program requires the attention of a full-time music director, that is not necessary in order to be celebrative. What is necessary is for all those creating the service to work toward the realization of something organically whole, serving a larger reality. And yes, the quality of the work matters. Music (or anything else) not done well embarrasses both its makers and its listeners. Still, the ultimate end is not to have "good performances" but to be one element that moves people from one place to another in their hearts and souls. That music, in turn, becomes an important ministry of outreach: it brings people to us; it binds us together; it feeds our souls.

One prospective member, drawn by the music offered by our church, recently said that to his great surprise, he finds himself talking about "my church" to his co-workers. "How can you not talk about music here?" he asked. Music becomes evangelism because it says "these people care about beauty; they care about the soul; they care about flesh-and-blood people."

Equally important, we must form a clear vision of what we celebrate/mourn, or otherwise experience in worship. A good illustration comes in our Unitarian Universalist attempts to deal with holy days in our worshiping communities. If we decide that our congregation will honor Christmas, then we need to look at the story and age-old meanings of the day and find what we can truly celebrate. Our task in worship is not to talk about Christmas, not to say how it should be approached, not to give helpful hints, but rather to celebrate its deeper meaning through story, song, and meditation. Our task is to call forth what we know about the divine born into the human. This is what we must do not only because integrity demands it, but because that is how we can serve.

Virtually everyone I've ever asked why they come to

church at Christmas identifies their reason as the desire to find some deeper meaning in the season. They want to see and hear beauty, to touch the sacred, to take a little bit of the magic with them. We do not serve them with half-aborted traditions, apologetic approaches, or hesitant theology. We serve them when we celebrate and recall them to larger thoughts. We serve them when we have the confidence fully to be what we are and fully to proclaim our message.

To serve those who come to us is an honorable thing to do. If they are served well, they too will want to act on their hope and love, and they, in turn, will serve the greater world. We will serve them so well that, finally, they will ask, "How can I not talk about my church?"

Excellence: Not a Passing Fancy But a Way of Life

Michael A. Schuler

OTHER COLLEAGUES may have visited more Unitarian Universalist congregations than I have, but after almost twenty years of service to churches in practically every region of the country, perhaps I have earned the right to make a generalization or two. The first is that a significant percentage of our liberal religious leadership—lay as well as ordained—doesn't fully appreciate the importance of quality and excellence as they apply to the physical condition of our churches. If they did, the facilities we Unitarian Universalists occupy would be far more attractive and better maintained than is frequently the case.

Having served in the past as a consultant to a number of congregations, I have had an opportunity to inspect a few of our physical plants. It never ceases to amaze me how conspicuous the disrepair and clutter can be. Concerned church leaders ponder the "secrets" of growth, and yet they fail to see what is as clear as the nose on their collective face: the chancel, the parlor, the kitchen, the classrooms are often a mess. My first piece of advice to more than one congregation has been quite literally to "clean up your act!"

Excellence

I have chosen to introduce this essay with a discussion of "appearances" because I think religious liberals have been prone to dismiss this issue as superficial. I, on the other hand, believe that a congregation's commitment to quality is first evinced by the way in which it anticipates the initial, gut-level reaction of the worshiper to the environment he or she is entering. Quality is not a goal congregations can pursue selectively or in a haphazard manner. One either makes a commitment to excellence—even in superficial things—or one does not.

Many of our churches have opted for quality in just one or two phases of their operations. They have developed an outstanding music program, lavish attention on "bricks and mortar," or support their minister's efforts to provide a scintillating sermon each week. I believe, however, that once excellence has become an explicit goal, the eyes of the congregation must be opened to the possibility of comprehensive, across-the-board improvement. Religious organizations should not promise too much nor attempt to do too much. But whatever is attempted should bear the mark of quality.

My second general observation is that "paying attention" is a precondition of excellence. If a congregation's buildings and grounds become unsightly, if its piano is out of tune or the sound system plagued by feedback, lack of maintenance money isn't usually the issue. The problem is that no one is paying close enough attention to such prosaic yet essential details to recognize and correct them.

Paying attention is not an easy skill to master, and in this fast-changing, multiplex world our focus is continually shifting from one concern or one interest to another. Because the church is peripheral to the lives of most of the laity, it is hardly surprising that they aren't more cognizant of its omnipresent needs. But someone *does* need to pay attention, and even over-committed lay people can be trained in proper stewardship if the church's leaders—especially its minister(s)—are vigilant. Too frequently the minister him- or herself is distracted, and, as a result, excellence isn't achieved.

Taking a page out of Wendell Berry's notebook, I suggest that a good minister is very much like a good farmer, and a well-run parish invariably reflects the dedication, the love, the intimate knowledge, and the skillful means of its proprietors. We can talk all we want to about "shared leadership," "lay empowerment," and "collective responsibility," but these principles don't mean a thing in the absence of a watchful guardian.

A parish minister's first object of concern must be the parish, even as his or her own fields and herds must dictate the schedule of the enterprising farmer. I suspect that high-quality churches are somewhat rare because too many ministers have cultivated a variety of outside interests that regularly pull them away, physically or mentally, from the parish. They are writing books and composing hymns, performing community service, or accepting denominational appointments. Such endeavors are no doubt worthwhile, but they ought not detract from the minister's primary responsibility, which is to encourage and foster excellence in his or her own bailiwick. We who are in this business need to be reminded sometimes that the local parish is where the religious rubber meets the road of life.

Like many of the Lutheran churches cited by Daniel Biles in his illuminating book *Pursuing Excellence in Ministry*, the First Unitarian Society of Madison, Wisconsin, doesn't get fancy, but tries to stick to the basics and do the basics well. We attempt to deliver a "package" of excellence that includes worship, education, aesthetics, and outreach, and I think we have prospered in recent years because our members have discovered more than one reason for being here. I suspect they also are proud to be associated with a quality enterprise.

Time may prove me wrong, but I have to believe that the success First Unitarian Society is enjoying has as much to do with the congregation's commitment to excellence as with demographic trends that have seen millions of baby boomers and their families drawn back to organized religion. I believe this is so partly because, being a boomer myself, I know that folks in my age cohort and with comparable experience and education aren't willing to settle for just *any* church. The men and women who visit the Meeting House are, like me, fairly discriminating; and they really aren't interested in a sloppy, slipshod operation. My peers don't accept mediocrity in their hospitals or in the schools their children attend. Why should they relax their standards when it comes to institutions that serve their spiritual needs? Wade Clark Roof makes exactly the same point in *A Generation of Seekers*, a recent inquiry into the religious dispositions and preferences of baby boomers. Many of those who are returning to church these days are accustomed to quality. On Sunday morning they demand more than a provocative sermon; they also want clean rest rooms, a decent cup of coffee, and considerate child-care.

By itself, however, good quality control will not push the average Unitarian Universalist church to the foreground in today's increasingly competitive religious marketplace. What we must strive for is excellence with *distinction*. We must lift up those qualities of Unitarian Universalist religious faith and practice that are unique and interesting and that speak to the needs of a particular subset of spiritual seekers. The First Unitarian Society of Madison has been successful in recent years, I suspect, because not only do we do things well, but also we do them differently.

The building we occupy is a case in point. My congregation is indeed fortunate to own one of the most distinctive and widely recognized worship spaces in the world—a structure designed by Frank Lloyd Wright. The Meeting House itself remains an object of significant appeal in the larger Madison community, and thousands of non-UUs tour our facility each year. For two decades, however, this Wrightian masterpiece was allowed to deteriorate, and as it fell into disrepair the congregation dwindled and its fortunes declined. It became obvious that although the landmark building served as a drawing card, it could not atone for a lackadaisical attitude on the part of its occupants. The very fact that the congregation had proven poor custodians of an architectural masterpiece spoke volumes to outsiders about the standards and priorities of local Unitarian Universalists.

Happily, First Unitarian Society's leaders finally awoke to the problem. Funds were raised, repairs were made, and the Meeting House eventually was restored. It is not entirely coincidental that the most rapid growth in the Society's history has coincided with the rehabilitation of its famous edifice.

Don't misunderstand me: it isn't the state of the building alone that has caused this reversal of fortunes. A new-found commitment to excellence, of which the physical plant offers the most tangible evidence, is responsible.

The conjunction of distinctiveness with quality has also been a hallmark of First Unitarian Society's music program. Not a few Madisonians were drawn initially to the church out of curiosity about the unconventional sort of music we often feature. In expressing what they like about us, people often mention our refreshingly different musical offerings and the fact that performers are not restricted to the canons of "sacred" music.

But again, it isn't enough to be "different." A stickler for quality, the Music Director at First Unitarian Society resists pressure from the congregation to have our fifty-voice choir perform weekly. Instead, the choir presents unusual and challenging works approximately twice each month. As a result, the congregation has come to trust that when the choir sings, the anthem will be truly special, not just another musical interlude. Furthermore, what is a treat for the congregation is also a morale booster for our largely amateur corps of musicians, most of whom derive great satisfaction from rehearsing and presenting difficult compositions.

Concerning that portion of the Sunday service under my control, I follow two cardinal rules. First, the entire liturgy should be uniform in quality. Preaching well is not sufficient. Too often, a well-crafted sermon is compromised by an injudicious choice of hymns, by trite or unpoetic responsorials, or by poorly edited, badly delivered readings.

My second principle is that every effort should be made to

prevent Sunday morning from becoming utterly predictable. There is, I realize, a certain value in maintaining liturgical consistency, and I do not believe a great deal is gained by abandoning wholesale a congregation's hallowed traditions. On the other hand, one of the distinctive features of Unitarian Universalist worship is that it attempts to create a meaningful synthesis of old and new, the traditional and the innovative. Liturgy that is too familiar fosters complacency; liturgy that is too obscure leaves the worshiper groping for familiar cues and landmarks. Quality Unitarian Universalist worship does not attempt to resolve this tension, but uses it to produce the desired state of "peace and unrest" in the worshiper.

In the context of Unitarian Universalist liturgical practices, I am moved to say just a word or two about the often-maligned "sermon talk-back" (called a "congregational response" in Madison). Many of our ministers have abandoned this practice either because they feel it compromises the worshipful mood or because they haven't figured out how to conduct a "poly-logue" that is cordial and unifying rather than argumentative and divisive.

I invite congregational response, not in all, but in some of the services I conduct—especially when the topic is sufficiently controversial to warrant feedback. I justify this practice on a number of levels: by permitting the open airing of differences, talk-backs dispel the image of the "pontifical" preacher; the insights and information brought to light frequently contribute to the congregation's understanding of the issues raised; I myself enjoy a bit of "jousting" with the congregation, and I sense that they appreciate the spontaneity of these public con-versations.

But most important, I see the congregational response as a practice that is distinctly ours, a liturgical device that dramatically underscores our historic commitment to reason, democracy, the toleration of differences. Newcomers to our church often remark on this convention, and express great enthusiasm for it.

Like anything else, of course, a congregational response can be conducted poorly or with flair, and if the worship leader lacks the poise to moderate such an exchange, it may be best not to make the attempt. Nevertheless, this is yet another fine opportunity for Unitarian Universalists to marry quality to uniqueness.

I conclude with an admonition: a parish minister's commitment to excellence can begin the process of reinvigoration, but it cannot sustain or complete it. The First Unitarian Society of Madison has proven successful because an entire congregation, clergy and laity alike, shares the conviction that our institution ought to manifest the liberal religious spirit in the finest manner possible.

Keeping the Ones We Raise

*Evangelism to
Our Children and
Young Adults*

Suzelle Lynch

PICTURE, in your mind's eye, a button—not the kind we use to fasten our clothes, but rather, the kind we use to declare our sentiments. Round, shiny, brightly colored, pin-backed. This button says, in print curved to hug its edge, "I was raised a Unitarian Universalist." And in the center, bold, bright letters declare: "I'm one of the 10%."

Some Sunday morning, take a look around your congregation. How many of the people there do you think qualify to wear this imaginary button? One in ten, one in fifteen, perhaps fewer? Do you know? Does it really matter?

I think it does matter. But perhaps that's because I am one of those people who could wear the button. My parents discovered the Unitarian Universalist church when I was four years old, and I spent thirteen years in UU religious education and then graduated from high school and spent ten years "out on my own," away from the church. Like many adult children of UU parents, if asked about my religion during those ten years, I would have claimed to be a Unitarian Universalist, but if asked whether or not I went to church, the answer would have been a resounding "No."

I outgrew that "No" when a search for like-minded folks, and perhaps some interesting single men, led me to darken the doors of a UU congregation at the age of twenty-eight. I met a lot of nice people in the church I joined, but much to my surprise, most of them had found the church as adults, and many of them were very new to it. I was shocked to find so few who were, like me, raised-up UUs.

Growing up during the sixties and seventies, near the tail end of the baby boom, meant I was surrounded by dozens of UU kids, even though my "home church" was a small, lay-led fellowship. As an adult returning to the church, I found myself wondering where all those kids had gone. Where did the hundreds of UU kids who went with me to junior high camp go? Where did the teenagers I hung out with at Lake Geneva UU Summer Assembly go? I asked around and was treated to the startling statistic that only ten percent of the members of our congregations were raised in our faith.

Now, on the one hand, this is good news about the appeal of the UU message. If ninety percent of us join the church as adults, we must have a religion that is very interesting and attractive. It also is good news for our future, for it means that we will continue to attract members to replace those who leave us, or who have lived out their years with us. I love being a UU, and as a minister, I couldn't be more excited that we continue to grow "from the outside."

On the other hand, I can't help but wonder why we don't seem to grow more "from the inside," too. I know some of us resist the idea of encouraging our children to join a UU church when they grow up, because many of us felt we had religion "crammed down our throats," and we don't want to do that to our kids.

It does make sense, this reluctance to proselytize our children. For if most of us have discovered Unitarian Universalism as adults, then perhaps we tend, on a subconscious level, to consider religion not as something to be developed from child-hood, but rather as something one has to journey away from one's upbringing to find, and then choose as an adult.

Our reluctance to proselytize our children also has its roots in Christian history. Beginning with the Council of Nicaea in 325 CE, most Christian sects have required an adult "conversion experience" before one is accepted fully into the communion of the church. Children, though they may be baptized, are not full members of the church until they covenant to be so as adults.

This is also true in most of our UU churches, fellowships, and societies. We no longer require proof of a conversion expe-rience, but the membership covenant is generally a function of signing the membership book and making a financial pledge. This opportunity is not usually opened up to children, though sometimes these days it is offered to teenagers after they com-plete a "coming of age" program, or UU catechism class, or affirmation class, as they are sometimes called.

Nevertheless, we do have, in the Unitarian side of our history, a powerful argument for birthright membership in our churches. This argument was made by the Reverend Sylvester Judd, a parish minister in Maine, in 1853. Judd, in a discourse that was to be presented to the assembled Boston clergy, suggested that children ought to be considered "birthright Unitarians," as a way of securing their Christian future. He believed that if more Americans were Christians, we would be a better, more civil-ized nation.

He pointed out that in his day only one out of ten Americans was a Christian (excluding "the Romanists," which was his term for Catholics) and that the practice of adult conversion to Christianity was different than the practices of Islam, Judaism, Hinduism, and other world religions, in which children are considered members of the faith community from birth, just as they are considered members of their families and part of their nations. Unfortunately, he died before he was able to make the presentation.

Judd harks back 200 years to the (Puritan) Cambridge Platform of 1648 to support his argument. One of the tenets of the Cambridge Platform is that the church consists of the believers and their children, in recognition of God's covenant with Abraham and his seed, forever after, as was written in Genesis 17.

The Puritan ideal was of a pure church in doctrine, polity, forms of worship, and membership—hence they separated from their parent church, founded their new community in the New World, and decided to accept only the "saved" into their midst. They did not like the idea that infant baptism admitted the infant into the church covenant, because this was too much like Catholicism, but decided that in accordance with God's covenant with Abraham, the infant became a member by virtue of its parents' covenantal relationship with the church.

However, what Judd didn't seem to realize was that unlike his concept of the "birthright church," these Puritan infants were really only "half-way" members of the church. They were not allowed to participate in the communion, the Lord's Supper, until they could furnish proof of a work of grace in their souls, that is, until they were saved. The children of these half-way members were also considered half-way members. Some years later, a Reverend Stoddard of the Northampton church opened up the communion to half-way members, which was a startling, but logical next step, and more in keeping with what Sylvester Judd would advocate 200 years later.

Judd had an interesting idea. Perhaps we do need to advocate "birthright membership" for our children. Consider what we lose when they grow up and "convert" to another faith, or become part of the great mass of "unchurched" in this country.

We lose important memories, the living record of how our religious education programs helped a young person become a vibrant adult. We lose energy, the kind of energy generated by a lifelong familiarity with our faith. We lose a sense of our history, of our roots, when every person in our congregations is "first generation."

It is true that our faith has always grown and stretched based on the needs and longings of those who join our congregations and that we receive many spiritual benefits from the many religious backgrounds we bring. But our congregations also benefit tremendously from the kind of grounding brought by those who have a lifelong knowledge of themselves as Unitarian Universalists. I do not mean to imply that one perspective is better than the other; we need both to keep ourselves growing toward wholeness.

We must think, also, about what our children lose if they are not encouraged to become a part of our congregations when they grow up. We spend hours of time and love in religious education classrooms, nurturing them along and helping them gain a deep sense of moral and religious values. They develop a deep sense of how valuable they are to us and to the world. Then when they become teenagers, things begin to change. Often our youth programming is patchy, and our kids lose interest. Or they dislike the "spill your guts" atmosphere of some of our youth groups and refuse to participate. And then they graduate from high school and most likely go off to college, and as a church we lose touch with them. It's not a glorious ending to a religious education process that begins with such care. It results in a loss of community, a loss of identity.

Conventional wisdom in our denomination, as well as in most mainstream Protestant churches, is that our children will return to the church when they have children of their own. It is true that this does happen from time to time. But more often than not, it doesn't happen, and I think our casual attitude is to blame. When we get right down to the bottom line, I think we need to ask ourselves, "What do we get out of being a part of this church?" We need to think about all the things we love about being here, and about our commitment to this faith. And then we need to ask ourselves, honestly, whether we want these things for our children.

Although we cannot be certain that they will come back as adults, we can be sure that they will be a lot more likely to do so if we let them know, from an early age, that we want them to! Encouraging them to take advantage of the benefits of a great church is very different than "cramming religion down their throats."

The best advice I've heard so far on this subject comes from a 1983 sermon titled "What Are We Doing to Your Child?" by the Reverend Tony Larsen, minister of the Olympia Brown UU Church in Racine, Wisconsin.

He says, "Tell your kids what you believe and why. And listen to their beliefs. And tell them why you belong to a church. And—heresy of heresies—tell them you hope they'll be Unitarian Universalists when they grow up, too. . . . There's nothing wrong with telling your kids you hope they'll keep up the good work."

Larsen also advocates teaching our children how to defend their beliefs. He suggests we make sure they know how to pronounce our name, and that we teach them a good, solid, easy-to-say answer to the question, "What do UUs believe?" Personally, I couldn't agree more. I have often wondered how much of my strong commitment to Unitarian Universalism today is due to having had to explain and defend myself, over and over, to my young Methodist, Lutheran, Catholic, and Presbyterian friends at school and pajama parties!

If we do wish to move in a more evangelical direction with our children, we also must realize that this will be experienced by some as a change in our institutional theology. The attitude that people will find us when they are ready will have to change, because encouraging our children to become UUs when they grow up means making ourselves and our churches readily available to them. It also means espousing a different attitude in our brochures and sermons—one that represents more often the viewpoints of those raised in our faith, as well as those who discovered it as adults.

One of the tenets of our extension program is that we need to have the structure in place to support growth before the growth occurs—I would stretch this metaphor a bit and say that before we can expect our children to join with us, we need to represent their voices in our pulpits. We need Sunday morning evidence that we are a church of raised-up UUs, not only a church of adult-UU discoverers. Our primary theology has been one of self-conversion; we need to change in the direction of a theology of cultivation.

Over the years, I have had many conversations with "raised-up UU" adults about what brought them back to the church, or about why they never left. I have also asked them if their siblings are active UUs, and if they're not, I ask what they think the differences were between their experience and that of their brothers or sisters.

On the surface, the reasons raised-up UUs seek the church as adults are no different than those of people raised in other faiths. Most often it is because they have had children and are looking for a religious education program. They also come seeking community, a place to belong, a source of spiritual sustenance and inspiration, involvement in social action or community service, and a way to meet people and make friends. The main difference is that those who were raised UU most often do not bring a lot of religious baggage with them. They come to our churches to affirm their childhood faith, not because they have rejected it.

But if I pursue the question of why they have returned to the UU church as adults one level deeper, the answers change. Almost every raised-up UU I have asked has pointed to an experience of feeling as though they were an important part of the church, or the larger UU community, when they were pre-adolescents or teenagers.

For one person, the pivotal experience was working hard—doing backbreaking physical labor—on a renovation project at a UU summer camp. For another, it was being asked (with the youth group) to lead the parade at the closing festival of a summer institute. Another person was the accompanist for her UU church choir, and still another remembers ushering and being asked and trusted to help count the money from the offering baskets. Having been known by one's childhood minister and feeling respected by him or her, as well as having the respect and attention of other important adults in the church, were also reported by raised-up UUs as significant in the decision to return to the church as adults.

Keeping the Ones We Raise

The teenage years are the pivotal time when we start to lose our children. As I'm sure many parents can testify, it is difficult to force a teenager to go to church on Sunday morning. Adolescence is that time when we start to take more control over our lives, and choosing not to go to church with the rest of the family can be an important way of asserting our individuality.

For many youths, church isn't what happens on Sunday anyway. Youth religion is the stuff of conferences or rallies, or youth gatherings at family camps or summer institutes, or Youth Caucus at General Assembly. In adolescence, religious identity shifts from religious education and family settings to feeling a part of a larger "UU youth tribe." For many of the raised-up UUs I've talked with, having had this tribal feeling also was an important factor in their choice to make the church home as adults.

Significant numbers of raised-up UU adults in our congregations have parents who are very active UUs. Believe it or not, parental modeling makes a difference! If the church is important to you, if you are seriously living your UU values—in congregational involvement and in the larger community—chances are greater that your children will choose to return to the church as adults, whether it be the UU congregation of their childhood or the one in their present neighborhood. Many raised-up UU adults also tell me that their parents encouraged them—perhaps gently, perhaps relentlessly—to come back and try the church as adults.

A third factor seems to be gender. I meet far more raised-up UU women than I do men. This speaks, perhaps, to the cultural notion of religion and church-going as a female province. Perhaps, too, we see fewer raised-up UU men because, at least in the heterosexual side of our congregations, they may marry women from other religious traditions, who have a stronger cultural obligation to affiliate with the faith in which they were raised. I say this tongue-in-cheek, but perhaps if we wish to see our children return in greater numbers to the church as adults, we ought to encourage them to pair up with other UUs!

And when our children do return, what will they find? If they come with their own children, looking for solid religious education, chances are they will be satisfied. But what if they are childless, or perhaps rather young (say eighteen to twenty-five years old), or gay or lesbian, or disabled? Will they find a church that not only speaks words of welcome, but that offers programming tailored for them? Will they find a church led by people with whom they can identify? Will their viewpoint ever be spoken from the pulpit on a Sunday morning?

I would like to speak specifically to the issue of young adult ministry, which has been defined as ministry with people aged eighteen to thirty-five. In some of our congregations, young adult ministry takes the form of a young adult group, which provides people aged eighteen to thirty-five with a way to meet each other and learn or socialize together. In some of our congregations, young adult ministry also means reaching out to the local university or college and including any raised-up UU students in church activities, as well as welcoming interested seekers raised in all faiths. In some of our congregations, young adult ministry is an intentional cultivation of younger people into church leadership and into volunteer jobs and activities where they can meet each other. But wherever it exists, young adult ministry is an acknowledgment that younger people, whether they are raised-up UUs or not, are important in the life of the church and that they have age-specific differences that call for a different ministry.

For example, consider the usual post-Sunday-service coffee hour. This is a time-honored tradition in most of our UU societies—the coffee is often free or charged for on the honor system. But for many young adults these days, the preferred caffeinated morning beverage is not coffee, but a diet soda. I have yet to see these offered, even as an alternative, at a UU coffee hour. It's a small thing, true, but perhaps symbolic of the kinds of changes we might make if we hope to welcome young adults.

I would also like to see our congregations begin a program of keeping in touch with our youth when they go off to college or to a first job. Even if they are thousands of miles from home and claim that they don't really want to hear from the church, I think we should stay in touch with them anyway. And I think we should contact the UU congregation nearest their school or work and have them added to the newsletter mailing list. A friendly phone call from a young member of the nearby congregation wouldn't hurt, either, nor would seeing news of their successful transition to the world of higher education or work in the home church newsletter.

Young adult ministry, whether it focuses on keeping the ones we raise or simply reaching out to all younger people, needs to be viewed as a denominational effort, one in which our congregations pull together. The young people we raise or nurture tend to be very mobile and may end up joining a church some day at the opposite end of the continent.

When I first came back to the church, I used to sit in the back row of the sanctuary and cry. I wasn't sure why I was crying, all I knew was that I had an almost overwhelming feeling of "coming home." The church I returned to was very different from the one in which I grew up; for one thing, it was almost ten times as big. But the sentiments being expressed from the pulpit were just the same, and they affirmed the beliefs I held most strongly and confirmed ideas I had held all my life. I knew I had found my place, and I wondered why I'd stayed away for so long.

And so it is that I think we need to tell our adolescent children something like this, "I would love it if you decided to stay and become a member of this church. It's also okay with me if you want to spend some time away from the church. But you also should know that I hope you will come back some day." And then we must get to work and prepare our congregations for their homecoming.

And who knows, maybe in a decade or three, we'll look around our congregations some Sunday morning and see imaginary buttons popping up everywhere that read, "I was raised Unitarian Universalist," with bold print in the center that declares, "I'm one of the 50%."

"Growing Times" for Religious Education

Barry M. Andrews

NOT LONG AGO, I attended a lecture at the Open Center in New York given by Martha Fay, author of *Children and Religion: Making Choices in a Secular Age*. The audience was largely in their thirties and forties and introduced themselves as teachers, spiritual seekers, and parents or would-be parents. Many also indicated that they were in interfaith relationships.

In response to the speaker's questions, almost all of those present revealed that they were looking for a religious alternative to the faith they had been raised in, something with spiritual depth and integrity, but without dogma and guilt. Many had experimented with other religions; some had joined various churches. They were motivated in their search by their own spiritual needs and by a concern for a religious upbringing for their children. Those in interfaith relationships were especially desirous of finding a religious community that offered a common ground for bringing together their religious backgrounds.

Most had not been involved in religious congregations for some time, but they had been feeling stirrings deep within themselves for "something more" than their personal quests had thus far produced. Parents in the audience felt that their children needed a faith to belong to and a place where they could find answers to "the big questions" of religion and ethics. Virtually everyone agreed that what they were looking for in a congregation was an affirmation of the individual's own personal religious search and the support of a religious community with a sense of identity and purpose.

After the discussion, as people were preparing to leave, Ms. Fay turned to me and said, "I know about the Unitarian Universalists. I interviewed a number of them for my book, and I have attended services at several Unitarian Universalist churches. Frankly, I am surprised your denomination isn't larger than it is. It seems to offer everything these people say they are looking for in a religious community." In her observation lurked a question about the growth of our movement: Considering our churches have so much to offer, why haven't we grown more than we have?

Unitarian Universalist congregations *have* grown in recent years. But why, considering there seem to be so many people who say they are looking for churches like ours, have they not increased in greater numbers? That's a difficult question to answer, not only because a number of variables are involved, but also because the answer requires a certain amount of soul searching on our part.

Partly, the answer lies in a certain resistance to growth in our congregations. Many church members fear a loss of intimacy or, in some cases, power, that an influx of new members seems to represent. There is also the threat of change—in our styles of worship, in our theological self-understanding, in our patterns of relating to one another—that a larger and more diverse congregation might entail.

I am not an advocate of numbers for their own sake. My own position is that if we continue to respond to the religious needs of our congregations, we cannot fail to grow. But that means we have a responsibility to offer quality worship and religious education and to make newcomers feel welcome. As a religious educator, I feel that religious education is especially important to our growth and vitality as a religious movement.

The people I encountered at the Open Center are not different from the people I have been meeting in the congregations I have served, and, if recent surveys are correct, they are generally representative of adults today in their thirties and forties, the so-called baby-boomer generation. In orientation classes and personal interviews with new members, the most common reason people give for becoming involved with a congregation is the religious education of their children. Increasingly, we are finding that adults are looking for religious education and small-group experiences for themselves as well.

My own experience is borne out in a survey conducted by Dr. Wade Clark Roof of the University of California at Santa Barbara. Dr. Roof describes the results of his study in *A Generation of Seekers: The Spiritual Journeys of the Baby Boom Generation*. Roof observes that after falling away from religion in their youth, increasing numbers of Americans are returning to the fold as adults. By far the most common reason given for their return is "for the sake of the children." Says Roof: "The presence of young, school-age children and feelings of parental responsibility for them drives boomers back to church to enroll their children in religious education classes."

The research indicates that only fourteen percent of single young adults have become reconnected with congregations, and the number only goes up to sixteen percent for married couples without children. But fifty-two percent of the returnees are married couples with children. Clearly, having children is the single greatest factor in the influx of new adult members in our congregations. This has resulted in a surge in enrollment in our religious education programs over the past decade. During my first three years serving the First Unitarian Universalist Church of San Diego, there was an increase of twenty-five percent in our church school and fifty percent in our youth program. In my first year here at the Shelter Rock Congregation on Long Island, there has been an increase of fifteen percent in our religious education program overall. Denomination-wide there has been a sizable increase in the numbers of children participating in our programs. Enrollment is up eighteen percent over the past five years, outpacing our growth in adult members. Clearly, in the words of the title of one of our religious education programs, these are "growing times" for our church schools.

Those coming to Unitarian Universalist congregations say they are looking for the same things parents told interviewers in the Roof survey that they wanted in a church school experience; namely, a religious education program that fosters religious identity and a sense of belonging, nurtures spirituality, provides an ethical framework, and helps parents and children answer the difficult questions of religion and life. Parents also say that they want a full-fledged program that offers opportunities for worship, community service, the arts, intergenerational activities, and play, as well as for learning in terms of religious education classes and curricula. It seems obvious to me that congregations will grow to the extent that they have such a program to offer.

Increasingly, parents say they want something for themselves as well. In this they are typical of many other adults joining our congregations who do not have children. Participants in the Roof survey frequently gave one or more of three main reasons for their returning to religious institutions. The first and most common reason, as we have seen, is to provide a religious education for their children. The second is to find a sense of meaning and purpose in life, and to discover answers to life's fundamental questions. The third reason cited is the importance of belonging to a community for mutual support, sharing faith, and pursuing common interests with others.

Many of the adults coming to our congregations today—singles and empty-nesters, as well as parents—did not have a traditional religious upbringing themselves. For large numbers of new members "church" is a novel experience. Because they were not raised in a church, relatively few come to Unitarian Universalist congregations with the sense of religious rebelliousness that brought so many to our societies in years past. Newcomers today are curious, open-minded, and intelligent. They are liberal in their theological outlook, eclectic in their spiritual tastes, and strongly committed to the principle of personal choice in religious matters.

Because so many were not raised in churches, they tend to share the ambivalent feelings of the unchurched in our society toward religious institutions. Moreover, they tend to be less religiously "literate" than those who, a generation earlier, had gone to Sunday schools in large numbers, even if they had a strong negative reaction later on. Still, they are motivated by a strong, if inarticulate, desire to address a religious void in their lives. Most visitors I talk with say they are looking for "a spiritual experience" and for a community that cares about them and shares their values. New Unitarian Universalists tend to be more comfortable with religious language and ritual than the "come-outers" of previous years. In fact, they are generally somewhat perplexed by the lingering aversion in many of our congregations to "God-talk."

For these reasons, among others, there is an upsurge of interest in adult religious education. Adults today want to learn more about Unitarian Universalism. They want to explore spiritual paths and examine other religions. They want to discuss ethical and social issues. They want to grow in their faith and their ability to meet life's challenges. And, especially in larger congregations, they want to meet and share experiences with others in smaller groups.

I would venture to say that if anything is growing faster in our movement than our Sunday schools, it's our adult education programs. In congregations offering well-organized adult programs, the response has been overwhelming. At First Church San Diego, for example, there was a 150 percent increase in attendance between 1988 and 1991. During the time I was there, the number of classes and workshops for adults grew from an average of twenty per year to more than fifty. San Diego is not unique in this respect. Judging by their brochures, other congregations providing comprehensive, well-balanced adult education programs are showing similar results.

"Growing Times"

Whatever their size and however they feel about the issue of growth, congregations should be assessing whether or not their religious education programs are currently meeting the needs of their children and adult members. Based on what parents today are saying they want in a religious education program for their children, congregations should be asking themselves the following questions in relation to their children's programs.

- *Does our program have a clear sense of mission and purpose?* Can we explain our philosophy and goals? Do our class leaders and religious education committee members know what the program is trying to accomplish?
- *Is our program strongly religiously identified?* Does it explicitly as well as implicitly teach Unitarian Universalist principles and draw upon UU sources? Do our children have a sense of belonging to a Unitarian Universalist congregation?
- *Is our program comprehensive?* Is our curriculum well-developed? Are our teachers properly trained? Does our program include intergenerational events and activities? Does it include worship for children and intergenerational services? Do we offer programs for parents? Do we have a summer program?
- *Does our program promote a sense of community?* Do children have friends among their classmates? Are new families made to feel welcome? Is there a sense of community in the program as a whole? How well do we integrate the religious education program in the life of the congregation as a whole?
- *Is our program child-friendly?* Is our curriculum engaging and age-appropriate? Is it fun as well as instructive? Is our nursery attractive and well-staffed? Do our classrooms reflect the interests of the children? To what extent does the motivation for their participation come from the children themselves?

- *Does our program deal with the crucial issues of life?* Does it help parents formulate answers to "tough" questions concerning values and beliefs? Does it help children to deal with ethical and social issues? Does it foster the development of faith? Does it encourage social action and community service?

Judging by what adults these days say they are looking for in the way of religious education for themselves, we should be asking ourselves a similar set of questions in regard to adult education:

- *Is our adult education program congruent?* Does it have a rationale and a plan? Are the courses offered part of a coherent program or just an assortment of classes? Is there a sense of purpose in relation to adult education?
- *Is our program well-balanced?* Does it offer courses in each of several areas, such as spiritual growth, personal development, life skills, and social issues? Are participants engaged in a variety of ways, emotionally and physically, as well as intellectually?
- *Is special attention paid to religious education?* Are there introductory, intermediate, and advanced classes on Unitarian Universalism? Are there courses on theology, ethics, spirituality, and world religions? Is there emphasis on personal reflection in addition to acquiring knowledge?
- *Do our programs foster a sense of community?* Are there programs and activities for a variety of interest groups? Are check-ins and small-group sharing a part of each class session? Do participants have an opportunity to socialize as well as learn?

The one absolutely essential ingredient of a successful, well-organized religious education program is leadership. Without dedicated, experienced lay and professional leaders, congregations will be hard-pressed to find positive answers to the questions posed above. In particular, congregations wishing to grow and meet the needs of children, parents, and other adults in the area of religious education will require the services of highly skilled and well-trained religious educators.

Unfortunately, there is considerable turnover in religious education leadership in our churches and fellowships, largely because of inadequate compensation and lack of benefits and support for professional development. The average tenure of directors of religious education in our movement is only about five years. Considering the importance of professional leadership in religious education, congregations are hampering the growth and quality of their religious education programs when they fail to retain experienced leaders.

The fact of the matter is that religious educators are, on the whole, very dedicated to their profession and that many possibilities are opening up for them in relation to their continuing education. Meadville/Lombard Theological School, through its Independent Study Program and resident courses, now offers graduate degrees in the field of religious education leadership. Other opportunities for professional development exist through the UUA Renaissance Program and membership in the Liberal Religious Educators' Association. Nevertheless, except in a limited way—primarily as ministers of religious education—a career path does not yet exist for the vast majority of religious educators in our movement.

Considering the importance of religious education in our congregations and the vital role it plays in attracting new members, we cannot afford to lose good religious educators. In fact we should want them to be better educated to deal with the needs of Unitarian Universalists of all ages in regard to religious education. Therefore, as congregations assess the comprehensiveness of their religious education programs and their desire for growth, they should also consider the adequacy of their compensation for quality leadership. Raising director of religious education salaries and offering benefits and professional allowances just may be the best single investment congregations can make in terms of their future growth.

Ten Working Principles of Unitarian Universalist Evangelism

Carolyn and Tom Owen-Towle

UNITARIAN UNIVERSALISTS have been reluctant missionaries given to periodic outbursts of low-grade evangelism. In recent times, however, we have begun to actively promote our religious cause for two simple reasons: *substance*—our life-affirming faith contains the most hopeful of good news to enhance a person's sacred quest and social witness; and *survival*—if we remain comfortably aloof yet unknown, we will erode into oblivion.

As a soldier in the Spanish Civil War would remind all purveyors of good news: "If you have principles but no program, you turn out in the end to have no principles." In our sixteen years of parish ministry in San Diego, we have found manifold programmatic ways to embody our Unitarian Universalist principles. Here are some working examples.

Hospitality Is Practiced

"Hospitality to strangers is greater than reverence for the name of God," says the Hebrew proverb, and the New Testament echoes the same sentiment with "I was a stranger and you took me in."

Ten Working Principles

Visitors venture bravely when they attend our Unitarian Universalist worship services. Even veterans, upon Sunday rising, must ponder: "Would anyone notice if I didn't show up today?" We think it is important to understand the tentativeness felt by the guest and the need for graciousness on our part as host.

Here, we are ever discovering, in surprising and workable forms, that the ritual bond of host and guest contains the consummate religious encounter. From the moment guests enter our gates until they exit the coffee hour, hosts greet and anticipate their needs. As the number of congregations in the county has grown to seven, we have labored to vitalize our growing cluster. We have many UUs represented now in district and continental leadership. We host a variety of associational gatherings. Our wintertime shelter program for homeless guests extends our hospitable outreach. We are all wanderers, passing through, guests of the universe, and our job as a religious clan is to share the earth's bounty and set a warm, inviting place for one another.

Beauty and Justice Are Interwoven

"Let beauty, truth and goodness be sung" echoes our church hymn every Sunday, followed by our aspiration, which unequivocally declares that "service is our prayer." As practicing Unitarian Universalists, we have neither the luxury of basking in beauty without leading lives of justice, nor attending to the needs of the oppressed while ignoring the unspeakable grandeur of existence. We are summoned to sing lustily from our hymnals and to serve the AIDS clients who use our premises. To minimize fruitless quarrels between the artists and the activists in our ranks, we remind both camps that beauty and service are equally holy adventures.

Some examples: our art gallery presents monthly shows, often with prophetic works geared to stir the conscience as well as spark the soul. Our music concert series schedules programs blending superior musicianship with steadfast commitment to causes of human rights and peacemaking. Not long ago, a renowned church organist, who had faithfully served a local Protestant church for years, was forced to resign for being gay. We wrote the church and organist of our distress at their action and invited this musical colleague to perform in our spring series. Whether the creative project be our handsome ceramic Memorial Wall that immortalizes our dead or the Wayside Pulpit, which remembers thoughts of Unitarian Universalist forebears and others with liberal sentiment, we require that both beauty and justice be exemplified in our creations.

San Diego's version of the Unitarian Universalist gospel aspires to build a community that occasions the restoration of our spirits through beauty and the reformation of society through service.

Our Religious Life Is Intentionally Diverse

On the front of our Order of Service is the phrase: "We Are An Intentionally Diverse Community." Actively, we welcome pilgrims of various races and classes, beliefs and orientations, to nourish their souls in our midst. Our place of worship is not called a sanctuary, auditorium, or hall but a "Meeting House." We wish to convey a spacious, inviting home where we gather to meet—to encounter self, neighbor, and God. Our spirits are invited to wander outward through a majestic, nature-filled window. The Meeting House creates a sacred crossroads where the depths of human experience and the heights of divine aspiration intersect through song, words, and silence.

The church is engaged in a number of persevering struggles for justice. A prime example has been evolving a supportive religious community for gays, lesbians, and bisexuals, many of whom are full participants in the programs and leadership of our church.

A broad programmatic embodiment of diversity is the San Diego Interfaith Gospel Choir, which got its start in our congregation in 1990 and has been housed here ever since. They perform during our worship services several times a year as well as throughout California. This choir adds a rich and diverse dimension to the church's choral program.

Ten Working Principles

The Interfaith Gospel Choir represents a coalition of the music committee and the Beyond Racism Task Force. It is robustly *interfaith*, bringing together at least six religious traditions including our own, and *interracial*, and is gradually becoming *intergenerational.* Each performance furthers our growing partnership in shaping a more diverse and inclusive community. Good music is an end in itself, yet the Interfaith Gospel Choir simultaneously incarnates prophetic witness and evangelism.

Gospel music delivers "good news" that reverberates with clapping hands and soaring spirits. We are learning that theological differences and cultural provincialism can be transcended through inspirational music and a shared commitment to create a more inclusive world. We are sometimes clumsy, occasionally tentative, even insensitive while pursuing our mission, but we believe that the fifty-member Interfaith Gospel Choir provides one way to lead us toward a society in which more people can come to know and trust one another.

Joy Fills the Air!

Our Memorial Wall carries this passage from Isaiah (55:12) as a reminder of our mission as a congregation: "For you shall go out in joy, and be led forth in peace; the mountains and the hills before you shall break forth into singing, and all the trees of the field shall clap their hands."

Laughter and playfulness, as well as seriousness and sorrow, flow in our community be it during marches or discussions, protests or parties. For example, as a UUA-designated "model congregation" working to create alternatives beyond gender violence, our local group's stated mission is "to create a sustainable community of greater gender justice and joy."

Theologian Ada Maria Isasi-Diaz once remarked that "the problem with you *gringos* and *gringas* is that you don't fiesta enough!" and social activist Emma Goldman vehemently declared: "I don't want to be a part of any revolution where there isn't dancing!" We dance a lot at First Church, with most of our dances being intergenerational and nonsexist; that is, we invite everybody to dance with everybody else.

The Stakeholders Bear Witness

Our church labors in several ways to make our gospel succinct, lucid, and compelling to both young and old, and to insiders and outsiders alike.

"Welcome to First Unitarian Universalist Church of San Diego—we are a community committed to the robust religious life that includes personal growth, social justice, and spiritual depth!" Some version of that mission launches every worship service and is followed by two immovable anchors of our common faith: the "Church Hymn" and "Aspiration," both printed in the front of the hymnal and sung and voiced in unison.

It is no coincidence that we call our covenantal statement an aspiration, not an achievement, because as religious pilgrims, we are finally activated, even measured, more by our hopes than by our accomplishments. The very words of our aspiration are also carved on two beautiful ten-foot sculpted ceramic pillars, *steles,* which greet, inform, and inspire people from the moment they enter our church gate.

We encourage laity from diverse constituencies in our congregation to share their personal affirmations during both worship services. These several-minute credos bear witness to the depth and breadth of parishioner's convictions as nurtured by our particular Unitarian Universalist religious community.

Inspirational readings, songs, and testimonies are part of all gatherings of our congregation, ranging from pledge-drive meals, social justice events, and adult religious education classes to business meetings. There is seldom a social or organizational event at First UU Church that does not begin with a reflective "check-in." This personal sharing both strengthens friendships and expedites the work that ensues. For us revelation and revolution are mutually reinforcing challenges.

Ten Working Principles

We have evolved a common symbol that is depicted on our church banner and captures a balanced commitment to the personal, social, and spiritual dimensions of our congregational adventure. On a banner is the tree of life superimposed upon the Tao symbol. In the midst of an incorrigibly yin-yang, para- doxical universe, we Unitarian Universalists are summoned to be living trees with a huge canopy of branches above and an unseen, yet vast system of roots below with a trunk that links these two growing networks.

As trees we have the ability to grow down, out, and up simultaneously. Our personal quest is sunk deep in the soil of history and community. The branches of our spiritual tree de- note compassion as well as extension. We reach out to shelter and house various fellow creatures. Our branches also extend outward via the establishment of three satellite San Diego con- gregations in the last decade. Our branches reach skyward in gratitude and yearning; they speak to us of transcendence and pay homage to the creation that nurtures us.

Members Are Comforted

We work to be a beloved fellowship. Toward that end, our Caregivers Network addresses the countless tasks of visitation, transportation, bereavement support, emergency housing, and meals. We consider the ministry of the church to be the charge and gift of all the members, lay and professional linked in ser- vice. Therefore, when people join the congregation, they are invited to assume an active caregiver role. Sound evangelism, we believe, is balanced by genuine gestures of *inreach* as well as *outreach*.

There are support experiences for singles and couples as well as for the women and men of our congregation, groups that meet regularly, not for therapy but for sharing and growth. In addition to nearly twenty current groups, laity and a staff Coordinator of Volunteers are ready to assist newcomers in forming fresh clans. In line with being an active Welcoming

Church, our affinity groups are open to persons of all ethnic backgrounds and sexual orientations. We also have "an extended family" program that comprises intentionally diverse, intergenerational clusters, usually no larger than sixteen to twenty persons.

A resolute commitment to community-building at First UU Church leads to frequent off-campus retreats for women, men, the entire church, and for various age clusters from the primary grades through senior high. Our own children and youth regularly schedule overnights on the premises. When expanding our buildings nearly a decade ago, showers were installed on campus for this purpose.

Worship services often include lay participation to explicate aspects of the human condition. Two of the most popular are the "Wholly Family" service, which honors many different configurations of families, and our "Transitions" service, in which significant life changes, such as retirement, graduation, divorce, vocational change, and illness, are shared through individual witness and congregational blessing.

As people gather for worship each Sunday, we are invited to silently light a candle in a sand-filled trencher to the side of the chancel. The candles are lit to mark sorrowful and joyous moments in our own lives and/or to uphold those about whom we care.

The Interdependent Web Is Embodied

The Unitarian Universalist Principles culminate with "respect for the interdependent web of all existence of which we are a part." In a historical sense, we declare allegiance to interdependence, ranging from the Unitarian phrase EGY AZ ISTEN ("God is one") to the Universalist claim that the entire creation is held in the embrace of an all-redeeming love.

Our practice has not consistently matched our theology. Historically, the Unitarian Universalist tendency has been to hallow solitariness over solidarity, rugged individualism over the intentional community, the independent will over the inter-dependent web. We treat freedom as a terminal rather than as an instrumental value, and our parishes make themselves suffi-cient unto themselves.

We have found here that our Unitarian Universalist "good news" is maximized when we embody the interdependent web as our dominant political reality. The majority of our more than sixty committees and organizations are co-chaired, often alter-nately convened, usually balanced with women and men. The Beyond Racism Task Force functions best when it is guided by both persons of color and whites, sharing interracial dialogue and alliance. All of our men's and women's support groups are gay, lesbian, and straight inclusive.

In our co-ministry we operate as a team of equals. As a result, women and men feel personally empowered to hand off, step back, move forward separately and together in the mysterious and exhilarating dance of shared leadership.

Our Community Is Evolving

L. B. Fisher wrote in 1921 that "Universalists are often asked to tell where they stand. The only true answer to give to this question is that we do not stand at all, we move . . . we are on the march." Each step of the religious journey holds some deepening affirmation, some correcting discipline, some fresh surprise. Evolution is not just biological and theological, but social as well.

We are an unfinished community, so everyone who enters First UU Church and joins in the odyssey is deemed an important contributor. As we state in our New Members' Litany: "We need you—your talents, your hopes, your resources—as you need ours. We believe that we are both blessed in this evolving covenant of membership." Those who are interested and ener-getic can move rapidly into leadership posts.

In an extremely mobile society, members come and go. Persons who leave us deserve to be recognized as well as those entering our ranks. So we have a Rite of Farewell during our worship service in which persons are fondly bid farewell then have the opportunity to voice their own good-byes and tell of future plans.

Loyalty Is Summoned

In everything we do, First UU Church attempts to help people deepen their commitment, not only to their special areas of interest but also to the overall church as an enduring institution. We teach the importance of creating and sustaining the mutual bonds of covenant. We promise one another allegiance through times of plenty and times of want.

This is reflected in the process of becoming a member. When joining the church, persons are encouraged to clarify and strengthen their individual decision through four stages: (1) meeting with someone from the membership committee to fill out biographical forms, ask questions, and receive an informative packet about the church; (2) meeting with one of the ministers to talk about their interests, what gifts they hope to bring to and what they can expect from the congregation; (3) meeting immediately after this with a member of the finance committee to discuss their pledge; and (4) participating in a formal welcome ceremony during a worship service that concludes with their signing the membership book.

Our Dead Are Remembered

Purportedly, there are two main reasons for joining a Unitarian Universalist community: to be able to speak and embody our truths and to be gathered unto our own (relatives and spiritual kinsfolk) when it comes time to die. Through the years the church has intentionally built structures and composed rituals that have paid respectful attention to those among us who have died.

One simple, yet enduring rite we use to honor a person's death is shared during the Sunday service. Brief words are spoken to capture the essence of the deceased person's character and to place them in our particular faith context. We extinguish our flaming chalice to signify their death, then light a separate candle to signify our ongoing memory of their continued legacy. "In mystery we are born, in mystery we live, and in mystery we die," conclude our words.

There are other markers for our deceased. Our Memorial Wall provides a timeless tribute to the members and friends of our families who have died—their names with birth and death years are imprinted in specially fired ceramic plaques. The names of those in our church who have died during the past year are read each Easter, followed by a litany of the names of the newborn. The garden around the wall is a place of meditation. The church has a canyon plateau from which we scatter remains. This is sacred ground.

Some years ago a fundraiser remarked that "one would hardly know that First UU Church had existed in San Diego since 1873, because you have so few markers indicating a history!" His prodding impelled us to start remembering our living and dead. Now, a number of rooms and objects have been dedicated, and we feel reassured by the presence of our spiritual ancestors.

We were inspired to name, during his lifetime, our chapel in honor of John Ruskin Clark, minister of the church from 1958 to 1977, currently minister emeritus. We are presently in the process of writing the history of our church, to be completed by 1998 for our 125th anniversary.

In a lovely garden near the church entrance stands a brick sculpture that holds a piece of circular glass etched with a flaming chalice. On a marble ledge is inscribed: "This Greeting Garden honors those who made possible the establishment in 1959 and the expansion in 1987 of this Unitarian Universalist center of spiritual freedom." It also quotes Christopher Wren: " If you would see their monuments, look around you."

Evangelism efforts at First Unitarian Universalist Church of San Diego are essentially guided by these ten governing principles.

Giving the Ministry Away

*The Role of the Minister
in Future Churches*

Barbara Wells

IN TALKING ABOUT ministry today, one never just means the professional clergy, but the mission and program of the church—its ministry. Ministry is certainly the most important aspect of any church. Yet ministry as we know it is changing dramatically and will need to continue to change if we are to move with strength into the future. How that ministry is changing was described best to me as "giving the ministry away."

I first heard this phrase when I had the opportunity to work with Terry Hershey, author of *Young Adult Ministry*, on a conference I helped plan through the Young Adult Ministries Working Group. Terry, through his experience as a singles minister at the Crystal Cathedral, a conservative Christian church of thousands in California led by Robert Schuler, learned the hard way about this topic. Because he couldn't "give the ministry away" he worked himself into burnout, losing both his marriage and ultimately his position. After swimming out of these depths, he realized the importance of and began to practice shared ministry. He, like many of us in both small and large churches, learned that ministry must move beyond the professional clergy if it is to be fully effective.

Giving the ministry away is crucial to the issue of growth in our churches. In this chapter, I want to explore a little of my perspective on this topic. After being a minister for nearly ten years and studying church growth for most of that time, I am convinced that we must look carefully at how ministry is approached in our churches if we are to effectively move into the future.

A paradox about churches has become crystal clear to me as I study large and growing churches. In these congregations, the senior minister must be strong, focused, and central—and he or she must share that ministry on every level. At Willow Creek, a nondenominational church in suburban Chicago and one of the largest churches in the United States, minister Bill Hybels is a constant presence and a strong leader. When I attended a seminar there, Hybels was ever present in all of our sessions, jazzing up the audience and sharing personal story after personal story. Most people found his presence to be enlightening and uplifting. In fact, many people attribute Willow Creek's growth (in 1994 still averaging over 15,000 adults at weekend services) to Hybel's personality and preaching.

Although Hybels is very much a presence at his church, the program and ministries of Willow Creek made it very clear that Hybels was not "in control" of every aspect of the community. With a talented staff and well-trained volunteers, the ministry extended beyond Hybels. In fact, they make it very clear at Willow Creek that ministry is what each member and each program at the church is about. Ministry is the heart and soul of that church for everyone.

St. Paul's Community Baptist Church in New York, whose story is told in the book *Upon This Rock* by Samuel Freedman, also gives us a model of an extremely strong leader. Johnny Ray Youngblood, their pastor since 1974, early on took that church in his hands, challenging the leadership and focusing its direction in the way he wanted. His preaching and presence were essential to its strength and growth. Yet you read over and over again in Freedman's book of the empowerment other leaders in the church received from Youngblood and each other. With so many programs and activities in the church, Youngblood discovered the importance of opening up the ministry to others. As he found himself sharing the ministry, the commitment of the people deepened, both to him and the church. What he was doing, and what is happening at Willow Creek, might be called empowerment.

Empowerment is a word that we hear a lot these days in reference to ministry. Many feminists and others have challenged the typical hierarchical model of churches and ministry. They invite us to share power across clerical and lay lines. I think what we are seeing in these large churches is empowerment, yet it is empowerment that does not lessen the professional clergy's standing. Giving the ministry away is like pouring water out of a cup that never empties. True empowerment means there is plenty to go around for everyone.

Why is empowerment important for large, growing churches? One answer is obvious. No member of the clergy can do every bit of the pastoral, preaching, teaching, prophetic, and organizational ministry in any church. Trying to control every aspect of ministry in a large church is impossible. Burnout becomes the name of the game pretty quickly. Burned-out ministers are sapped of vitality and hope. And ministers without these two attributes are not likely to lead a church growth revival.

But there are other reasons why giving the ministry away is such an important part of church growth. Too often, people who are put to work in our churches, say, on a committee, find themselves unhappy with the mundane aspects of the day-to-day duties of keeping a church afloat. One of the wonders of Willow Creek is that every task done, every group that meets, every committee that organizes, understands itself as a part of a ministry. Even the people who come together to trim the shrubbery are a part of a grounds ministry. They see themselves as gardeners for God and take time before powering up the lawnmower to power each other up with prayer and sharing.

Giving the Ministry Away

Certainly, Senior Minister Bill Hybels isn't out mowing the grass with the guys. But you can be sure he is in contact with the staff minister in charge of that program. The grounds ministry is just one of many at Willow Creek. Not only are there the ministries we might expect for children, youth, and families, but also young adult ministries, singles ministries, even parking lot and pizza ministries are active. No job in the church is too unimportant to be considered a part of the greater ministry of the church.

It may seem hard to think of pizza making and car parking as ministries. But ministry is, I believe, the work and service a church offers to its members and to the world. When a person sees parking a car for a visitor as a ministry, they are much more likely to view themselves and the person they are helping as in relationship. And it is in relationship that holiness is found and God is known. I didn't like everything I saw at Willow Creek, but I do think that seeing every function of the church as a ministry empowers the people in tremendous ways.

Obviously, maintaining a huge program, building, and staff as they do at Willow Creek requires an enormous amount of communication. The lines of accountability are therefore crystal clear. Everyone knows to whom they are connected. Hybels, in his role as senior pastor and spiritual leader of the church, stands in the middle of this great web of connection. His gift has been one of real personal and spiritual presence in the pulpit as well as having an abiding trust in the people who share the ministry.

So, giving the ministry away means sharing not only the pulpit, like many Unitarian Universalist ministers do gladly through lay services, but also all aspects of church life with the volunteers who are the church. If we look at the models of Willow Creek and St. Paul's, we can see clearly the work of the church as a ministry. Both leaders empower staff members to do their work while remaining accountable to each other and the senior minister, and they make sure that everyone doing ministry is well prepared and trained.

I believe we have a lot to learn from these models. Certainly few of today's liberal clergy were trained in seminary to share the ministry. Most of us have been trained to work out of a pastoral, lone-ranger model, seeing ourselves as doing the ministry for everyone. Most theological schools do not teach ministers to work collaboratively with each other or the laity . Yet when we give the ministry away, wonderful things can happen. One of my favorite stories about large church growth is a fine illustration of just this point.

Some years ago a minister of a large church was sitting in his living room watching the evening news. To his horror, he heard a news report that the son of a family in his church had just been arrested for a brutal murder. Immediately, the minister got in his car to go see his beleaguered parishioners whose son was now in jail. When he arrived at their house, another church member stood at the door keeping the press at bay. They let the pastor in, and he saw another church member on the phone answering questions and fielding calls. Another couple was just arriving to take the couple's younger children out for a few hours. And yet another couple sat in the living room with the parents. As the pastor walked in, he reached out to the couple and said, "What can I do?" They replied, "Pastor, the church is already here for us."

Because this minister had given the ministry away, these people were far better served than if they had expected him to do it all. His church members not only responded to the crisis, but they also responded lovingly and appropriately. We must assume they had been trained and supported in their ministry of care to one another. That had been the minister's job far more than just showing up at the doors of people in trouble.

Although this aspect of shared ministry is by far the most important for church growth, I want to look at one more important issue. Giving the ministry away is not only about techniques, it's also about style and attitude. When clergy feel free to share the ministry with others, this attitude is likely to spread to other areas of ministry. One such area is worship.

Leading worship services has been the job of the professional clergy for centuries. Worship was and continues to be central in the life of any church. Preaching is crucial to helping people enter into the life of a church community as it is through the "word of God" translated through our lives, that individuals help to see how they are connected to the holy and thus to each other.

I had an inkling about issues related to preaching that were confirmed for me not only by Willow Creek and St. Paul's, but also by a long conversation I had with Tony Robinson, senior pastor of Plymouth Congregational Church in downtown Seattle, Washington. Plymouth is an established church with close to 1,000 members. Services have an attendance ranging from 300 to 400 a week. Not "mega," but on a par with some of the larger Unitarian Universalist churches.

I talked to Tony because he had written an article about Willow Creek in *The Christian Century* some years ago. Tony, like me, visited Willow Creek to see what it had to teach him about the modern approach to church. I was curious to hear how he brought his learning about this mega-church to bear at Plymouth. Worship, he told me, was key. As a biblical, old-style preacher, he enjoyed and felt comfortable with intellectual, carefully researched, and well-written sermons. After visiting Willow Creek, he realized that if young people were going to come back to his church, he was going to have to change his style. Younger people, Tony discovered at Willow Creek and through conversations with people at his own church, were hungry for truths about their own lives that could be measured against his. No longer would he be the preacher, high and lifted up with no doubts, no personal losses, no anger or shame. Rather, he began to trust himself to tell some of his own life to his people. He gave up a pristine manuscript for notes and stories. He tried to imagine the Bible characters as real-life people doing real-life things. And he asked himself, "Does what I have to say matter to the everyday, ordinary person trying to work, raise a family, and still find meaning and happiness in life?" If their answer was no, he threw it out.

This approach to preaching, highly personal and practical, is clearly the model of most mega-churches. It is much more appealing to baby boomers and their younger siblings. Why this is, I'm not exactly sure. Tony, in his article, was reminded by his experience at Willow Creek that most people "are concerned about personal worth and meaning, family relationships and simply coping with life. Instead of assuming that most of us are all okay and perhaps wish to become somewhat better, Willow Creek assumes we are broken and need healing." ("Learning from Willow Creek," *The Christian Century*, January 23, 1991, pp. 68-70) This approach to people rings very true to me.

Preaching then, becomes more emotive, but it need not be mushy or flowery. If you read any of the sermon material in *Upon This Rock*, you can see clearly the style Johnny Ray Youngblood learned to trust. He speaks of his own wild youth from the pulpit, not bragging but not apologizing either. He is who he is, and his preaching is clearly authentic. And his people love it.

We Unitarian Universalists still have some trouble with this approach to preaching. Most of us were taught to be intellectual preachers, and I know I still feel a little guilty if I preach a sermon without reading a book first or writing out my manuscript word for word. Yet every sermon I preach that comes from my heart and personal experience, seems to touch people far more than the ones taken from books. I believe the religious climate of today begs for us to dole out, to put a spin on Emerson, "thought, passed through the fire of life." Growing churches, within our movement and beyond, have worship services that are highly personal, practical, moving, and spiritual. To change in this direction is hard for people, I know. But I believe it is not only practical to do so but spiritually right.

Giving the ministry away begins with an attitude toward church life that sees in everything we do the potential for ministry. It is acted out through shared leadership, empowered laity, and through the very act of preaching itself.

My research has taught me, and to some degree my own

Giving the Ministry Away

experience bears out, the need to change significantly the way we practice ministry. Learning to give it away, empower others, and trust our own spirit to preach the word are just part of what I have learned. I believe that as we move toward a new century, we will discover even more.

Responsibility and Commitment

*Why Just
"Signing the Book"
Is Never Enough*

Barbara Wells

I HAVE HEARD a story in some form in many a Unitarian Universalist congregation across the continent. It is an innocent story that tells a lot about how Unitarian Universalists perceive the importance of membership.

Joe and Judy Everyperson visit Anytown Unitarian Universalist church. They are church shopping, trying to decide if they belong in a liberal religious community. Following the service, they decide they'd like to at least get on the mailing list, so they sign the guest book they find on a table in the foyer.

A few weeks later, after having church shopped some more, they join another church. A few months later, they are contacted by someone from Anytown Unitarian Universalist church for a pledge during their every member canvass. When they tell the canvasser they haven't attended in months and that they joined another church, the canvasser protests, "*Our* records show you joined Anytown four months ago!"

Turns out Joe and Judy Everyperson had signed the membership book instead of the guest book.

When people tell this story to me, they generally laugh, thinking it somewhat funny. But I wonder, is membership in our churches so unimportant that people can be on the books for months without anyone knowing or caring? Is belonging so casual that the membership book can land in the foyer for anyone to sign at any time?

So I challenge people to tell me what it takes to become a member of their church. The replies vary, but the theme is similar. Far too often in our churches, to join one need only "sign the book." No class or interview necessary. No pledge required until the fall canvass rolls around. No expectations of involvement. No commitment to learning and growing in faith. In essence, to join our churches one simply has to show up and sign the book. You can then disappear into the crowd never to be seen or heard from again (and many do).

My intent in writing this chapter is to challenge this norm of lightweight commitment to membership in Unitarian Universalist churches. In my experience casual commitment to membership translates into indifferent support for the church in all areas from volunteerism to financial support. Serious commitment, I have discovered, usually translates into real involvement at all levels. This kind of commitment and involvement eventually evolves into more active and engaging congregations. And active and engaging congregations attract people.

Donald Smith, in *How to Attract and Keep Active Church Members*, affirms this. His book speaks of the concept of "bonding churches," churches that have both high growth and low loss of membership. He believes that "the temptation for most mainline churches is to make it too easy to join a church . . . [yet] high expectations . . . promote congregational vitality." The expectations may vary from church to church, but unless they are clearly articulated, growth is less likely to occur.

Growing churches are churches where high expectations and serious commitment are the norm. If we are to grow our

Unitarian Universalist churches for the future of our movement, we need to heed this call.

What might high commitment look like in a Unitarian Universalist setting? When I first began learning about church growth, I asked myself this question. Many people attracted to our churches are freedom-loving individualists. It has been said that leading a group of Unitarian Universalists is like herding cats. Many Unitarian Universalists resist hearing about commitment because to them it smacks of creeds and dogma. "I'll be a member if I choose—don't tell me what I have to do to join," some of them have been heard to say.

Nevertheless, although this has been a common theme in Unitarian Universalists who joined our churches a decade or more ago, many of us are finding that it is less true in the newer and younger members of our churches. Baby boomers and their younger siblings and even their children are much less concerned about these issues. Perhaps because these generations have been given so many choices, they take freedom more for granted. They have freedom, now they want commitment and community. I believe they go hand in hand.

My experience of creating a new church at the beginning of the 1990s has shown me that most of our membership (who are primarily boomers) were eager for guidelines about what membership means. They wanted to know, and were clearly willing to do, what was asked of them if they understood its importance. During my years of exploring the importance of membership, I developed, with the help of many others, a "Path to Membership" class that clearly delineates the responsibilities of membership. The Path to Membership class is required of all people interested in joining our church. In it, I spell out the responsibilities of membership in a Unitarian Universalist church:

1. Attend church regularly
2. Work on your own spiritual development
3. Serve on a task group

Responsibility and Commitment

4. Pledge at a stewardship level
5. Be involved in service to others
6. Connect to the wider UU movement

Let me provide a more detailed description of what these responsibilities entail. The first is simple: attend church regularly. Simple, but often neglected in our approach to membership. Although we cannot expect people to attend every Sunday, it is certain that if you don't attend services on Sunday, you are not likely to feel yourself a part of the religious community. Communal worship is extremely important to the life of any church. If you do not partake of it often, you are less likely to feel connected to the spiritual heart of the church.

For parents with children in the religious education program, this responsibility is even greater. It is hard enough to help children understand the importance of Sunday school without making it harder by sporadic attendance. Children gain far more from the "context" of religious education than the content. If they are not there regularly to experience the community first hand, they are not likely to want to keep coming back.

The second responsibility on our path to membership is that each of us will work on our own spiritual development. Unitarian Universalists have no creed or dogma. We believe that each of us is capable of discovering religious truth as it is revealed to us in our lives and within our church community. It is imperative that we take responsibility for our own spiritual well-being with the support of the church.

As church members, we have the opportunity to partake of the many aspects of the church that might enhance our spiritual growth. From worship services to teaching Sunday school, the church should be providing places of religious connection and nurture. But even if it isn't, as religious liberals we cannot just wait for spiritual growth to happen. If we call ourselves Unitarian Universalists, we are called forth to seek truth and spiritual connections in all we do and all we are. Church membership should be clear on this point.

Third, when joining a Unitarian Universalist church, new members should understand that the many tasks and activities of the church community are not done for them but by them. A responsibility of membership is to do tasks associated with the church. These tasks may vary from the simple (serving coffee on Sunday) to the sublime (chairing the board of trustees), but all the tasks are important.

Congregational polity, including the reality that the church governs itself and looks to no one "higher up" for rules and creeds, requires of us our hands as well as our hearts and minds. Although most churches are clear that they need help from members if they are to function, not all are willing to require it of people. Yet when we are absolutely clear what we are asking of members, most will gladly step up to the plate. Why join a church if the expectation is not there that they participate?

Related to this is the fourth responsibility: stewardship. The financial support of most of our churches comes almost entirely from members. Unitarian Universalists are notoriously poor givers. Despite our statistical affluence, Unitarian Universalists have a lot of trouble understanding the importance of what has been called, "sacrificial giving." Sacrificial giving asks us to reflect on what we might need to give up in order to support our church. It asks us to be careful stewards of the church, not just give a "token" pledge. Unless we help people understand this important responsibility of membership, most new members will stay on the fringe of the community, not giving of their resources to support it.

Stewardship is key to Unitarian Universalist church growth. We can articulate a message of hope and the potential of the human spirit to create a holy and whole community on earth, but unless it is held up by simple stewardship the church will disappear. Unitarian Universalists cannot be coerced into giving money. We cannot hold up the threat of eternal damnation if our members don't give. But I find that people do understand stewardship if they are given the opportunity. Rather than running away from money issues, our churches can learn to speak the gospel of our liberal faith in conjunction with its support. When we do, the support is there.

In the new congregation I helped to start, we kept financial issues open from the beginning. We talked about how much it cost to run a church and spoke directly to each member about their responsibility. Although not all of our members were initially comfortable with it, most accepted it as healthy for our church after one or two canvasses. People understand that by being members they must commit their treasure as well as their heart. And most give until it feels good.

We give in many ways, and the fifth responsibility of membership underscores this. To be a member of a Unitarian Universalist congregation, each of us must commit our faith to action. In other words, we are called as liberal religious people to show through our works what we say with our mouths. I make it clear in the Path to Membership class that these good works do not necessarily have to happen at church. Although the church provides (we hope) opportunities for social action, many places exist in each of our lives where such acts can take place.

Most Unitarian Universalists are readily accepting of this responsibility. In fact, many come to our churches because they want to be in a church where people "walk their talk." Yet I find that by articulating these acts as a responsibility of church membership, people begin looking at their acts differently. They are given permission to see these acts of caring as deeply religious and as an essential part of belonging to a faith community.

Finally, the sixth responsibility is to connect to the wider Unitarian Universalist movement. Congregational polity is a powerful and wonderful aspect of our religious lives, but one negative side effect of it is that it often keeps us from feeling that we are a part of something larger than just our own church. Too many Unitarian Universalists are "First Churchatarians" only and do not truly commit themselves to the religious movement of which we are all a part.

By telling people clearly that this connection is essential to their membership, it encourages them to look beyond their own church to see the many churches and Unitarian Universalists "out there." I tell new members that by simply reading the *World* magazine, they will feel themselves a part of something wider and bigger than our church can hold. If some of them want to get involved at deeper levels in the movement, this gives them encouragement to do so.

Becoming a member of a Unitarian Universalist church can be one of the most important things a person does in his or her life. Membership in our churches should be considered a sacred responsibility and never be taken lightly or for granted.

After people join, the importance of membership can be continually affirmed. A welcoming ceremony during the worship service is a must. Many churches use a litany that involves the new members and the entire congregation. Some churches put new members' biographies in the newsletter or the Sunday order of service. Others have a new member speak for their "class" at a Sunday welcoming service.

My primary intent in this chapter is not to look at how to assimilate new members, but I can't stress its importance enough. New members become "seasoned" members when they are included in the activities and life of the church. Churches need many places for people to connect. More and more, people are looking for social and spiritual engagement. Committee work, while essential to running a church well, cannot replace the power of really getting to know someone at a deep level. This kind of knowing takes place best in an affinity group or class, not at a committee meeting.

For Unitarian Universalism to move with strength into the future, we must begin to ask more of ourselves and each other within our churches. When people commit themselves to something, their lives can be transformed. I know, I've seen it happen. Over and over again I have met people who, before entering the doors of any Unitarian Universalist church, felt that their life was missing something very important. Once through our doors, they discover what it is they're lacking—spiritual community. If they are given the tools and the maps for the journey into a committed relationship with their church, the odds are good that they will stay and grow with the church. If they are not challenged to be truly committed members, they might easily slip away once the thrill of arrival wears off.

When I imagine our liberal religion in the future, I see active and committed members at Anytown UU Church. When Joe and Judy Everyperson enter the doors of this church as visitors, they are welcomed with joy and shown exactly where and how to sign the guest book. When they are ready, they will be given the membership book to sign. No one will confuse the two, for they will understand that membership in our church is a precious and wonderful responsibility.

Slaying Dragons of Hate
with Ribbons of Love

Marilyn Sewell

I TOOK UP MY POST as the parish minister of the First Unitarian Church in Portland, Oregon, in August 1992. I had no idea of what I was walking into.

One of the first persons I met was Peter Blumklotz, husband of our moderator, Joyce Blumklotz. Peter was up and around, but was beginning the long, slow process of succumbing to liver cancer. It was Peter who handed me the "Fight OCA" button, almost before Joyce introduced him to me. "Here," he said with a grin. "You'll need this." He was right. OCA stood for the Oregon Citizens Alliance, the organization that was working mightily to pass Ballot Measure 9, a measure that purportedly would prevent gays and lesbians from having "special rights." In fact, the measure would remove certain civil rights from gays and lesbians and would declare homosexuality to be "perverse." I still have the button. It reminds me of Peter. And it reminds me that, although Ballot Measure 9 failed, the "Son of 9" is already in the works for our next election here in Oregon. It's a watered-down version, and it could very well pass.

No sooner did I walk into the church office that August

Slaying Dragons of Hate

when I was greeted by Kathy Oliver of Outside-In, a social service agency for homeless teens that is located in a building on our church property (thanks to the vision of former minister Alan Deale, we own the whole city block on which the church sits). Many of Kathy's clients have left home, or have been driven out, because of their parent's disapproval of their homosexuality. Kathy said that she would like to call a press conference and tie a red ribbon around the entire block, declaring it a hate-free zone. What a beautiful and simple concept! I l usted in my heart to claim the idea as my own—although I could not, but at least I knew a good public relations angle when I saw one. "Yes, of course," I said. "Let's do it!"

I did not go to the Board of Trustees for permission. I did not go to the congregation. I mean, what could anyone possibly say in opposition—"I'm for hate?" Our national organization had, of course, years ago declared our denominational stance on equality for gays and lesbians, and one of our Principles and Purposes states that we believe in the worth and dignity of all people. It is important to know that our stance makes us different from even the most liberal Christian churches. We were the only church in town who could make such a witness. The Presbyterian minister just down the street from us agreed wholeheartedly with my stance, but had he wrapped a ribbon around the Presbyterian block (they own one, too), he probably would have been, symbolically at least, strung up by that ribbon. As it was, he lost two pledges that year, totaling $100,000. As I told my congregation later, I wouldn't have to worry about losing that kind of money from two pledgers no matter what I do. (Nervous laughter—they know just how true that is.)

The press conference took place at noon one day early in September. The kids from Outside-In had climbed on ladders all that morning wrapping the block with red ribbon. (What kind of ribbon? I'm often asked. It was the waterproof red warning ribbon used on construction sites. After all, this is Portland, Oregon, where we do expect rain from time to time.) They also put signs up at various anchor points along the ribbon, signs proclaiming, "Hate is not a family value," "Hate Free Zone," and other such sentiments.

The media began to arrive, and soon we had three TV stations, two radio stations, and a reporter from the newspaper. Kathy and I were to give speeches, as was Pauline Anderson, a councilwoman who is a member of First Unitarian. Before noon, a small crowd had gathered to cheer us on. By chance, the Women's Alliance was having its first luncheon meeting of the year, and when they heard what was going on, they all trooped out and joined in. This group is composed mostly of elderly, establishment-looking women, the white-glove set, and so you can imagine the legitimacy and power of their presence and their voices at this event. Several were interviewed and sent their message of justice into the living rooms of Portlanders that evening on the news. (Can your grandmother be wrong on an issue like this?)

I thought carefully about my speech. I wanted to address it to people who might be on the fence about this issue, good people, who as practicing Christians may have been told that "the Bible condemns homosexuality." I wanted also to let the community know who we Unitarian Universalists are and what we value. I wanted them to know that we are a church that not only talks the talk but walks the talk. I wanted unchurched liberals out there in TV land to know that ours was a church that they could join forces with if they wanted to defeat the OCA and Ballot Measure 9. And I wanted gays and lesbians in the community to know that they would be welcome at the First Unitarian Church and that we would stand in solidarity with them against those who would attempt to demean and diminish them. The following is the text of that speech:

I come here today because of a grave concern.

The state of Oregon, long seen by the rest of our country as progressive, has of late been the setting of hate crimes, bigotry, and intolerance. Ballet Measure 9 asks us to legislate bigotry and intolerance, to give it the status of law. Here today, we are doing the reverse: we are declaring this entire block, which is owned by the First Unitarian Church, as a hate-free zone. Here you are welcome, whether you are black, white, Asian, Hispanic, or Native American. Here you are welcome whether you are Jewish or Christian, Buddhist or humanist, atheist or agnostic. Here you are welcome, whether you are gay or lesbian or straight. Here you will be treated with the full measure of respect and dignity that every human being deserves.

I want to say a word to those people who believe that homosexuality is evil—that it is unnatural and contrary to the will of God.

In the first place, as my gay and lesbian friends have explained to me, their sexual orientation was not a decision but a discovery. At some point in their lives, they realized they were homosexual. In other words, they were simply made that way. The decision is whether to hide that fact, for fear of reprisal, or to admit to themselves and to others their true orientation and try to live out of that honesty.

In particular, I want to speak to those who see themselves as Christian and claim a Christian basis for their rejection of homosexuals. In the New Testament Paul does write against homosexuality (Romans 1:26-2:1, Corinthians 6:9-11, and I Timothy 1:10), but remember that Paul was against lust and sensuality in anyone, homosexual or heterosexual, because he was afraid that these feelings would keep a person from putting God first. Homosexuality is not mentioned anywhere in the four Gospels. Apparently, Jesus was not concerned about it as a moral issue. However, Jesus was very much concerned with self-righteousness, with condemnation of others, with injustice. Jesus was an advocate of the poor and of the downtrodden, of the "unacceptable" people in his culture—the Samaritans, for example.

Jesus stood for love and stood against hate and discrimination. Should today's Christians do any less?

Today we tie a ribbon around this block. We say welcome to all. We say all are deserving of love. We say all are deserving of justice. In declaring this a hate-free zone, we hope that the beautiful city of Portland, the great state of Oregon, will also be increasingly hate free, a place where tolerance and diversity are a way of life, a place where justice is a given, a place where love and neighborliness flourish.

What was the result of the ribbon-tying event? It's impossible to measure, of course. I don't know to what extent people's thinking may have been shifted, if at all. I will tell you what I observed about changes in church attendance, though. Gays and lesbians in the community began to get the word out: First Unitarian welcomes us, cares about us. And many began coming to services. It is important to understand how vicious and intimidating to homosexuals the political climate was at that time. Can you imagine how it must feel to actually have a state vote on whether or not you are perverse? Some gays and lesbians were threatened with bodily harm, and in fact a gay man and a lesbian woman were actually killed in a fire bombing incident during this period. More than once I held someone who was weeping as he or she went through the line to shake my hand after a service. "Thank you for making this a safe place for us to worship," some said. Although Portland is progressive in many ways, that is not true of all her citizens, nor is it true especially of the smaller communities in the state. The skinheads/neo-Nazis have chosen our state as their headquarters.

The word got out to others in the community as well—people who were looking for like-minded folks to worship with and to join in working for justice in various forums. Our membership grew an astounding forty-one percent last year, again something I never bargained for. But it happened. I can't say what all the factors were, but I know that it was not because of anything we did to recruit members. We didn't even have a membership committee. We still don't send letters to visitors. I don't think we're particularly friendly to visitors. If the truth be known, we don't even know who the visitors are most of the time. I am not proud of these things, and we are slowly organizing to do better—but our energies are mainly going into coping with all the people who are attending in spite of our slipshod attentions to them.

Let me hazard a few guesses as to why all this growth has occurred. One obvious answer is the demographics—Portland is a rapidly growing area. And then some of the new folks are simply old members who had dropped away and who came back to check out the new minister. This is a phenomenon that always occurs when there is a change of ministry. Some of the growth occurred because we made the membership book accessible and invited people to join. It's a simple act, but an important one: Invite people to join. They should, of course, be apprised of the covenant of membership that they are agreeing to, should they make this decision. It's not just signing the book: It includes pursuing spiritual growth, giving service, and making a financial pledge.

I heard a speaker from the Alban Institute say that the single most important factor in church growth is having a strong and very visible identity. I think this element is crucial to our growth. Now we are known as "the church who wrapped the ribbon around the block." Others know this of us, and we ourselves refer to that time with particular pride—it is a symbol of the best that we are. I hold it up before our congregation to let them know of the importance of our witness, a liberal witness no other church can give quite so readily or so well. The heading for our advertisement in the Saturday paper has been changed to read "First Unitarian Church, a Liberal Voice in Downtown Portland." These words are important in the largest city in a state that is the most unchurched in our nation and in a city in which liberal thinkers are often disdainful of church people as hopelessly conservative and out of touch. That is because, for one thing, the conservatives make the most noise. They are the ones who largely funded Ballot Measure 9.

And one other thing about the growth: When somebody asks me, "Why are so many people coming to your church?" the short answer I give is "erotic energy." Let me explain, lest I be misunderstood. I'm using the word *eros* as it has been redefined by Audre Lorde and subsequently by other feminist thinkers, such as Carter Heyward and Rita Nakashima Brock: It signifies the source of our creative energy, something close to *elan vital*. I'm talking about the celebration of life. I'm talking about joy. This past year, I visited two mainline churches here in town, interested in seeing what was happening. Nobody laughed in either service. The hymns were like dirges. Never mind the theology—I couldn't imagine attending either church regularly, for no other reason than I got little sense of life, of vitality, from either.

First Unitarian is a joyous, celebrative church. By that, I don't mean we don't take on hard issues, because we do—a recent Sunday worship service was on AIDS. Even with something this devastating, however, there is a measure of joy and peace in knowing that we are a community and that, because we are a community and not isolated individuals, we have all been affected by this disease; and we stand in solidarity with those who are most deeply affected. That is our "good news": We love, and we believe that love is stronger than death. Easter is coming soon. There it is again. You can't beat love, you can't beat life as a message.

The "Son of 9" will be on the ballot again this year, and we will be an even stronger voice saying, "No!" Perhaps another ribbon will go up, the way they are going up now in other parts of the country, for example, in our UU churches in Cincinnati and in Kansas City, where the forces of hate are hard at work. Ribbons recall to me my childhood when my mother braided my hair and tied the braids with ribbon. Ribbons of youth, of innocence. Ribbons on May Day poles. Ribbons tying gifts or holding flowers for the beloved. Fragile things, these ribbons.

Slaying Dragons of Hate

But strong enough, because they are tied with the hands of love.
Strong enough to slay the dragons of hate.

About the Contributors

Barry M. Andrews is both a parish minister and minister of religious education who was ordained in 1981 and currently serves as Minister of Religious Education at the Unitarian Universalist Congregation at Shelter Rock, New York.

John A. Buehrens has been a parish minister since 1973, has served churches in Dallas and New York, and currently serves as the President of the Unitarian Universalist Association.

Charles A. Gaines has been a parish minister since 1961 and has served as the Director of the UUA Department of Extension.

John E. Giles has been the lay minister of music at the First Unitarian Church of Evanston, Illinois, since 1991.

Harvey M. Joyner, Jr. has been a parish minister since 1978 and currently serves as the minister of All Soul's Unitarian Church of Colorado Springs, Colorado.

Robert W. Karnan was a parish minister from 1970 until his death in 1995 while serving as Senior Minister of the Unitarian Universalist Church of Portsmouth, New Hampshire.

Tony A. Larsen has been the parish minister at the Olympia Brown Unitarian Universalist Church in Racine, Wisconsin, since he was ordained in 1975.

About the Contributors

Suzelle Lynch is a graduate of Starr King School for the Ministry and has been working in ministry with young adults since 1988.

Suzanne P. Meyer has been a parish minister since 1983 and currently serves as minister of the First Unitarian Universalist Church of New Orleans, Louisiana.

William Burnside Miller was a parish minister from 1973 until his untimely death in the spring of 1994 while serving the Unitarian Universalist Church of Fort Meyers, Florida.

Susan Milnor has been a parish minister since 1987 and currently serves as co-minister of the First Universalist Church of Minneapolis, Minnesota.

John C. Morgan has been a parish minister since 1984 and currently serves as the district extension minister of the Joseph Priestley District of the UUA.

Thomas and Carolyn Owen-Towle have been parish ministers since 1967 and 1978 respectively, and currently serve as the co-ministers of the First Unitarian Church of San Diego, California.

Lawrence X. Peers is both a parish minister and minister of religious education. He was ordained in 1987 and currently serves as the Director of Education and Research of the UUA Extension Department.

Michael A. Schuler has been a parish minister since 1976 and presently serves as minister of the First Unitarian Society of Madison, Wisconsin.

Carl G. Seaburg is a parish minister and historian who has served the denomination in a variety of capacities since his ordination in 1945. Though technically "retired," he continues to work and write.

Marilyn Sewell has been a parish minister since 1987 and currently serves as senior minister of the First Unitarian Church of Portland, Oregon.

Brent A. Smith has been a parish minister since 1984 and currently serves as co-minister of All Souls Unitarian Church in Tulsa, Oklahoma.

Arvid Straube has been a parish minister since 1979 and currently serves as minister of the Eno River Unitarian Universalist Fellowship in Durham, North Carolina.

Barbara Wells has been a parish minister since 1985 and currently serves the Unitarian Universalist Church in Woodinville, Washington.

Scott W. Alexander is a native of Wisconsin, and a graduate of Lawrence University of Wisconsin and the Starr King School for the Ministry. Ordained as a parish minister in 1974, he served the First Church of Houlton, Maine, from 1974 to 1978 and the First Unitarian Society of Plainfield, New Jersey, from 1978 to 1988. From 1988 to 1991 he was the Minister/Administrator of the Church of the Larger Fellowship, Director of the UUA Office of Lesbian and Gay Concerns, and Director of the UUA AIDS Action and Information Program. In 1991 he was called to become Senior Minister of the Church of the Larger Fellowship. He is the author of *The Relational Pulpit: Closing the Gap Between Preacher and Pew*, and the editor of *The Welcoming Congregation: Resources for Affirming Gay, Lesbian, and Bisexual Persons* and *AIDS and Your Religious Community: A Hands-on Guide For Local Programming.*